Etheldreda

Princess, Queen, Abbess and Saint

To my wife Patricia and all our family,
and to all who value the legacy of Etheldreda

Etheldreda

Princess, Queen, Abbess and Saint

by

Norman Sneesby

Fern House

An original paperback first published in 1999 by
Fern House, High Street, Haddenham,
ELY, Cambridgeshire CB6 3XA

A catalogue record for this book
is available from the British Library

ISBN 0 9524897 8 3

Jacket by Chris Winch Design
Printed in England by TJ International Ltd, Padstow

ABOUT THE AUTHOR

 Norman Sneesby was born on the family fruit-farm in Wilburton, a village on the 'island' of Ely. He attended the village school and the local grammar school, where he excelled in athletics and cricket.

From there he went directly into the RAF; by the end of the war he was flying on operations with Coastal Command. At the University of Reading he won the Prize for Geography in 1950, and later went on to obtain an MS (Agric Econ) at the University of California at Berkeley. As a principal research officer with the Ministry of Agriculture at Cambridge he headed a team concerned with land use problems and land quality appraisal. A Fellow of the Royal Geographical Society, he published several articles, and delivered lectures, on soil erosion and other agricultural topics. As a side-line he planted – with the help of his wife Patricia, their two sons, family and friends – a two-acre vineyard at Wilburton, one of the first in the country; he recorded the story in *A Vineyard in England*, published in 1977. The wine was called 'St Etheldreda'.

On his retirement he and Patricia indulged their long-held desire to travel to far-flung places. For several years he imported wine, and opened a specialist wine shop in a converted cart-shed. Recent years have seen his return to Ely and much involvement in the life of the city and its cathedral.

Norman Sneesby considers himself a true countryman by birth, upbringing and inclination, with a strong allegiance to his locality and to Ely itself, which he regards as the ideal of a country market town.

Seventh-century England was an unstable mixture of feuding kingdoms, a cauldron of warfare in which Augustine's new religion struggled to survive. Into this turmoil was born a child named Etheldreda who, through the remarkable events of her suddenly-ended life, was to become the most popular female saint in the whole of Saxon Christendom.

This is the story of a dedication, and a succession of dramatic episodes which were to put her commitment to the severest test. It tells of terrible happenings and the triumph of Etheldreda's physical and moral constancy and courage, and of the culmination in an epic and fearful journey back to her beloved island rising like a vision above the fenland swamps, and how Etheldreda founded a great monastery which in the fullness of time was to become the magnificent cathedral of Ely.

ACKNOWLEDGEMENTS

In the preparation of this book many people gave me factual information, advice and encouragement. I am grateful to everyone, and particularly to the following: the Bishop of Ely; the Archdeacon of Wisbech; the Dean and Chapter, and members of staff, of Ely Cathedral; clergy and members of the churches of Exning, Haddenham, West Halton, Stow-in-Lindsey, Minster, East Dereham, Lindisfarne, Bamburgh, and St Etheldreda's at Ely; staff at Hexham and Ripon Cathedrals; Mr Dennis Bedford, Braham Farm; Mr R G Parish, Bedwell Hey Farm; archaeological officers at Sutton Hoo and St Abbs Head; the Curé at Faremoutiers in Brie, France; the Sisters of the Benedictine Abbey at Faremoutiers; Mrs S Smout; Miss P Blakeman; Mrs J Burgoyne; and, as always, to my wife Patricia for her support and encouragement. My special thanks go to Zoë Dale for handling the text and the illustrations.

The front cover is derived from an eighteenth-century stained glass window of Saint Etheldreda in the Bishop's House at Ely. I photographed this with his kind permission, and I acknowledge with thanks his agreement to its use in the preparation of the cover design. Through the window can be seen a fine birch tree, standing, as its predecessors may have stood, within the precincts of Etheldreda's seventh-century monastic foundation.

Note: All photographs within the book were taken by the author, who also prepared the maps and the drawings.

The old lane at Wilburton.

CONTENTS

ILLUSTRATIONS

MAPS

PREFACE

Just below the crest of the ridge runs a quiet grassy lane, grooved and scarred with the seasons. There are tumbling brambles and great trees on its lower side, beyond which once lay my father's plum orchard. This thoroughfare is over two thousand years old.

Adjoining the lane on its northern fringe are Bronze Age burial mounds, and over to the east there existed – people will tell you – a Roman villa. Very close to the trackway on the southern, downhill side, a spring-fed well is always filled with cold, clear water. I was born in Springwell Cottage, and in my early years the hillside spring supplied all our needs. The ancient lane followed a narrow outcrop of sandy soil, where trees and bushes had been readily cleared and the land was easy to till. Below it the slope becomes gentler, and all the way along the contour runs a spring-line, where the sand laps over the lower clays. The rain falling upon the clay ridge flows over its surface and is lost in the sand, gushing forth at its feather edge below. Always there was a source of good water, and hutments were built along the spring line. A little further to the west the monks of Ely dug a line of five fishponds, each fed from the one above; they are there today, the nesting places of moorhens.

This lane of great antiquity was trodden by Celts, Romans, Anglo-Saxons. It would indeed have been much used by the seventh-century Saxons, for it provided an open route from the settlement at Cratendune, and later from the great church at Ely, to the village of Haddenham. There at Haddenham was the hall of Ovin, governor of the island of Ely, while in the monastery at Ely dwelt its foundress Etheldreda. She and her steward Ovin had worked together for many years; they had enjoyed the good days and suffered together through times of trial. Now Ovin had died, and in his village Etheldreda erected a great cross of stone to his memory. This monument, the cross-piece itself lost and the base now in Ely's cathedral, stood about a mile from the location of our Wilburton cottage and my father's orchard, which lay across the southern slope of the ridge and patterned it with the snow-white blossoms of early spring.

How many times must Etheldreda have travelled along this ancient route to meet and talk with her great servant and even greater friend? Perhaps their meeting place was by the springs of our own homestead, when Etheldreda was a young princess and he her steward, and all those years later when she was in middle age and the monk Ovin was very old. And in between had come the length of Etheldreda's strange, almost unbelievable story.

For years I have been convinced of a physical link between the site of the smallholding and the life of our own island princess, later to be the first abbess of Ely. The orchard, and the vineyard which replaced it on my father's retirement, have gone for ever but in my own mind the mystique of their situation will always remain.

In walking west along this old green drove one makes a slight detour and then returns to the original crossing of the ways, and it is here that the mounds of the Bronze Age burial stand within ancient pastureland. One lane, now extinct, ran below the curve of the ridge through to Ovin's residence, another dropped down to the edge of the fenland morass, and the third climbed to the ridge top and thence straight to the church. This church was built in medieval times, and a new village pushed out along a high road which ran to Ely so that the older settlement, now redundant, was left to decay.

Within the church is a Victorian window dedicated to St Etheldreda. When, with my family, I planted the vineyard we had a year or two to decide on the name of the wine and it was when I looked again at the superb window within the church that the name came clearly to me: the wine would be called 'St Etheldreda'. It was good wine and won many prizes and I wrote a book telling the story of the vineyard. The label was illustrated in the book and when I wrote the chapter entitled 'Our Saxon Princess', with a short life story of Etheldreda, my interest in her extraordinary history was rekindled.

Later – much later – I became a guide at the cathedral of Ely and found myself talking to visitors about Etheldreda's life and, once more, the fascination returned and would not go away. What sort of person was she and what made her react to happenings, and take actions, in the way she did?

I found myself wanting to bring this apparently enigmatic person to life in the form of a story which would not only embrace a detailed factual history but also try to question and to analyse. It seemed to me that the nineteenth century writings were often shallow, ill-considered, sounding no ring of truth. I have studied chronicles, dissertations, articles and maps and tried to piece things together into a coherent whole; and I have visited places from Faremoutiers in France to Coldingham on the Scottish coast, from Sheppey to Rendlesham and across to the two Stows of Lincolnshire. I have some knowledge of physical geography and soils and of agriculture and rural life, and an abiding interest in the personalities of history, but the qualification I value most is an advanced age during which not a few of the ways and experiences of life have been absorbed. Some may disagree with the scenarios I have brought forward but, in my eyes at least, they make a fair degree of sense and they do bring us an Etheldreda we can understand and to whom we can relate.

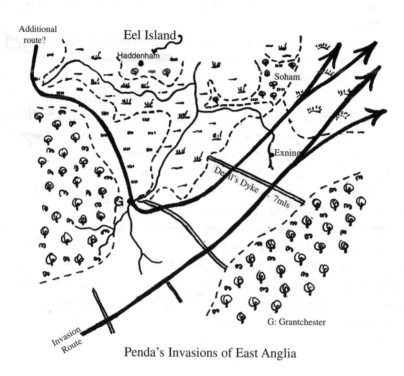

Penda's Invasions of East Anglia

1

THE OUTPOST

Etheldreda, Princess of East Anglia and the island of Ely, Queen of Northumbria and Abbess of Ely, was born in the year 630 in her father's residence at what is now the village of Exning in Suffolk. Today's Exning is modest in size and very much involved with horse racing. In the seventh century its local shopping centre, the town of Newmarket, did not exist but in medieval times the 'old market' at Exning was supplanted – probably due to a plague – by the 'new market' on higher, better-drained land a couple of miles away.

Etheldreda's father Anna – the name in broad translation from the Anglo-Saxon can be taken to mean 'Unity' – was a prominent member of the ruling family of the Kingdom of East Anglia. He was a nephew of the great King Redwald, who had his main seat at Rendlesham, near the present town of Woodbridge in Suffolk. The Rendlesham buildings stood on dry sandy land close to an inlet of the sea, perfectly placed for trade with the continent. The Exning palace, by contrast, was sited in a stream valley, surrounded by open chalk hills. When Anglo-Saxon settlement came to be contemplated this sheltered little hollow, with clear fresh water, good fishing, lush grassland for cattle, and trees for fuel would have been an obvious choice. The Celts had earlier used the valley as a tribal meeting place before the Anglo-Saxons arrived and drove them from their homes. To the invaders the site was an ideal one; they were valley dwellers by nature. But why would a nephew of the King want to live here, fifty miles from the royal headquarters by the sea?

The answer can only lie in the fields of politics and of warfare. and particularly the latter. What we now know as England was divided into seven kingdoms of which East Anglia, though perhaps the richest, was only one. The dense forests of East Anglia were separated by a line of open chalk uplands from a tract of impassable swampland and beyond, over to the west, was the Kingdom of Mercia, soon to be governed by the implacable Penda. Even before he came to the throne in 626 Penda the warrior was much dreaded by his neighbours. Resentful – he never forgave a slight, real or imagined – and ferocious, he was said never to have lost a battle, and he seemed only to be content when engaged in the bloodiest of warfare. The plunder of wealthy East Anglia for the appeasement of his heathen gods would have provided a driving motive – or perhaps simply an excuse – for leading his men along the wind-blown ridges of chalk which were from the earliest times the route into the sandy heartland of East Anglia. Once into the vast tract of wild open country we know as the Breckland men could be mustered in their thousands, ready to track downstream along the gravelly river meadows, ransacking villages and slaughtering their inhabitants, and so reaching the sea where, if the crucial battle against the East Anglian king had not already taken place it would be fought out at Rendlesham itself.

It was therefore essential that the narrow tract of chalk land be held at all costs if East Anglia were to survive, and someone of power, authority and skill had to be there to keep an eagle eye on any signal which might mean an imminent invasion.

At this time there was a series of parallel 'dykes' built across the downland, extending between the forested clays and the impenetrable marshes. No one knows how old these ditches might have been by the seventh century; they could have been created by the Celts and renewed by the Saxons, but recent investigations have suggested that the Saxons themselves threw up these four great defensive works. Each successive one was a deep dry ditch filled with brush with, on the northeast side – the side to be defended – the diggings of earth thrown up into a high bank with its crest reinforced with sharpened stakes, behind which a reserve of men could assemble at short notice to face an attack. The sole point of weakness would have been the causeway through which access had to be maintained between one ditch and the next and along which, in peacetime conditions, trading traffic could roll its way through and up into East Anglia.

With these considerations in mind, the secondary 'palace' – more, in truth, a military advanced base – was set up in the fertile Exning hollow, no more than two miles behind the final and most formidable ditch, still existing today as the Devil's Dyke. And here it was that Anna, an intelligent leader of men, would have been charged with defending the Kingdom.

Anna's residence – however it may be described – would have been a simple rectangular hall, wooden-planked with a thatched roof, with small rooms perhaps partitioned off within the building. Outside would have been all the paraphernalia of a military base: huts for the soldiers and their supporters, weaving sheds, artisans' units, enclosures for horses and cattle, and so on. One imagines that the army, standing in reserve for the most part, occupied themselves on the land, with sentries manning the palisaded banks ready to sound an alarm at any time. Anna would probably have had his spies on the Mercian border – men who knew the tortuous pathways through the fenland and followed them to report regularly to Anna.

Although basic in construction, the royal seat of residence would not have been too uncomfortable a place in which to have been brought up, particularly as it was sited in idyllic countryside. Though the hall itself was rudimentary, soft furnishings of all kinds would have hung from the walls, carpeted the wooden floors, and been draped over the tables and chairs, cheating cold draughts and providing comfortable resting places, while the beds would have been covered with warm furs. The bright colours of the materials, the shining metals of the jugs and goblets, the treasured ceremonial pieces, would have reflected the winter log fire, ever burning in the middle of the hall, to produce a feeling of well being – albeit a somewhat smoky one – among those lucky enough to have been born within the royal family.

Etheldreda was one of these fortunate few. She was born at a time of peace. That peace was soon to be disturbed, but for a few years at least the borders with Mercia were to remain quiet. The great King Redwald had lived by his wits, treading a fine line between traditional paganism and the new Christian religion which had been introduced into Kent by Augustine and transmitted, however tenuously, into East Anglia. On Redwald's death, probably in 624, his kingdom reverted to paganism. What this meant in practice was that the royal court re-embraced paganism; the ordinary people in their villages would have simply followed their rulers or, more likely, been totally unaware of conflicts of belief, struggling as they were with crop failure, incessant fires within the villages, frequent accident and injury, and ever-present disease. Their short lives beset with hardship, they had little or no time to reflect upon matters of religion, and they pursued their wearisome ways almost akin to those of the farm animals upon which they relied for milk, meat, leather and fur.

This great defensive ditch, embanked on the East Anglian side, would have been even more pronounced in the seventh century.

We have seen that Anna was given the responsibility for the defence of the ditches. Who charged him with this task we cannot know, but one may believe that King Redwald, as he grew older, chose to return to Rendlesham to live out his final years and picked as his western commander the best man for the job. Sigbert his younger son could have done it, and done it well, but Redwald had fallen out with him and sent him to France. Eorpwald, his dynastic successor, was still at that time a pagan like his mother, and was perhaps just as likely to accept Mercian domination as to oppose it. Anna was not in line for the throne, and not subversive by nature. Moreover he had always leaned towards the Christian faith, though he had taken no formal vows; certainly he would have had no dealings with pagan Mercia.

So in the year 630 we see Anna at Exning with his wife and their then four children: three daughters and a son. Things were quiet along the ditches: Penda, Mercia's most powerful warrior, had only recently become its king while Sigbert, a noble and upright man and a strong Christian, had commenced his reign – in equal measure just and popular – over the kingdom of East Anglia. It was a good time by the standards of the day for the child Etheldreda to be born, to live out her infant years by the clear running stream, to play amid the meadows and woodlands and, before long, to join with her whole family in baptism into the Christian faith, by the springs sparkling their way through the copse which, secluded and mysterious, exists to this day.

2

FAMILY TIES

Redwald's devout son Sigbert finally returned from his French exile to become king, but he was a reluctant ruler, and having rescued his nation from paganism he yearned to pursue his Christian studies and hand over the crown to someone else. But his next-in-line cousin Egric – elder brother to Anna – though well-meaning, was indecisive, and Sigbert felt it in the interests of the nation that he himself should handle its affairs at least for a few years. And there came a tranquil interlude in East Anglian life, only to be cut short in 640 with an invasion by the great Mercian leader Penda which resulted in the death in battle of both Egric and the now-retired Sigbert; hauled by the people from his monastery to replace the useless Egric, Sigbert had faced the Mercians with only a symbolic wand. It was now, when Penda withdrew to confront a Northumbrian menace, that Anna became king of East Anglia. But all this was to take place a decade from Etheldreda's birth, and in those early years the prospects for peace were still looking good.

Anna had married a lady whose name is lost to us. Bede says that she already had a daughter called Sethryd, and we know something of Sethryd's later life. She went, like many young Saxon women of noble families, to northern France to study and to take the veil, there being at that time nowhere in England where a woman could do this. Her actual destination was the abbey at Faremoutiers-en-Brie, a 'double' monastery for monks and nuns. Here she did very well and succeeded the great French Abbess Fara in 655. This was considered especially creditworthy since she was not French born. She was now a person of great monastic experience, and mature in years – probably in her forties. However she was not to remain Abbess for very long; she died sometime around 660.

The secluded chapel near Faremoutiers, in the French province of Brie, is dedicated to Etheldreda's sister Ethelburga.

The king had another daughter who duly migrated to the same monastery in France. She was called Ethelburga, or 'Noble Stronghold', and seems to have emulated Sethryd throughout their two lives, becoming in her turn Abbess at Faremoutiers. Ethelburga appears to have been a very determined person. As Abbess she sought to build an additional church dedicated to all the Apostles, but its construction was proving disastrously expensive. Nevertheless Ethelburga decreed that its building should be carried on despite the protests of her subordinates, and it was only on her death in 664 that the work was abandoned. Like Sethryd she became a saint, and in France is much revered and known as Ste Aubierge.

Somewhere along the family line came a son named Iurminus. There was once, behind the high altar in the abbey of Bury St

Edmunds, the shrine of St Jurmin, who is undoubtedly the same prince. Apart from the information that he was killed in battle alongside his father in 654 (and may have been originally buried with Anna at Blythburgh), Iurminus remains a mystery, but it is a reasonable guess that, like other royal sons, he would have spent most of his time being schooled by his father – the more so when Anna himself became king – in military prowess and managerial skills.

But if upon the child Etheldreda – 'Noble Power' – her brother Iurminus made no real impact, while Sethryd and Ethelburga remained remote if much respected rôle models, it was a very different story with her sister Seaxburga.

Seaxburga, 'Guardian of the Seax' – the short dagger from which the Saxons derived their name – was older than Etheldreda; this is clear from her marriage to the young King Erconbert of Kent, perhaps a couple of years after his accession in 640, the year Etheldreda was ten. Erconbert, by this marriage, entered Etheldreda's family as her brother-in-law. Probably little more than twenty when he succeeded his father, he was grandson to the great High King Ethelbert who reigned for no less than fifty-six years and was converted to Christianity by Augustine shortly after the latter's arrival in Kent in 597.

We do have one clue to Erconbert's character and that is his royal decree that all pagan idols within Kent should be destroyed forthwith. This was quite revolutionary – even Penda had permitted freedom of worship – and does perhaps indicate that here we had a particularly forceful young man, very much with the courage of his Christian convictions. He would have been totally supported – even prompted – by Seaxburga, whose Christian beliefs were indisputable. It must have been a sound marriage between two people of exceptional personality and it is hardly surprising that their daughter Ermenilda had sufficient strength of character to follow Seaxburga as Abbess of Ely. Ermenilda had been married to a new Christian King of Mercia and had taken the veil when her husband, in the manner of so many, had died on the battlefield. (Erconbert was an exception to this bloody rule; he died in the plague of 664.) And Ermenilda's own daughter Werburga became the fourth, and the best known throughout the England of those days, of Ely's early Abbesses.

The marriage of Princess Seaxburga to King Erconbert of Kent would have been of the greatest importance to both kingdoms. Each, despite East Anglia's immediate troubles, remained wealthy and now, after brief reversions to paganism, well settled into the Christian faith, one with a mature and potentially powerful king in Anna; the other with the prospect of a long reign under a very positive and clear-minded man whose only need now was for a wife and children. Soon after Erconbert's accession, therefore, would have come the arrangement of this marriage, promising a long union between the two nations and linking East Anglia with the cultured Frankish kingdom of Erconbert's grandmother. Penda, now the Mercian king, was still very much tied up in Northumbria but he was likely to pose a further threat to the two southern kingdoms before long, and alliances had to be forged without delay. Seaxburga would have been the obvious choice, indeed probably the only one. She was the sole East Anglian princess of marriageable age – fifteen or sixteen – who had as yet taken no decisions about her spiritual future.

Seaxburga seems to have been a singularly healthy and energetic person, raising a large family, carrying out her duties as Queen of Kent, later founding a monastery at Sheppey and becoming its Abbess, and ultimately succeeding her sister at Ely and taking steps to translate Etheldreda's body into the monastery there.

It remains to reflect upon the influence Seaxburga must have exercised over her younger sister. An age difference of four or five years would not have precluded a very close association between the two daughters – though this would of course have been only sporadic once the elder one had become Queen of Kent. Up to the time when Etheldreda was eleven or twelve – in other words during her most formative years – Seaxburga would have been all-important to her, a crucial influence on her early life. Seaxburga's devotion to, and affection for, her younger sister seems to shine through Etheldreda's story, and as the second and long-time Abbess of Ely she is awarded much veneration.

Exning church stands on a low hill above water-meadows, and quite possibly marks the exact place where Etheldreda was born.

But what of the influence of their mother, of whom we know nothing except that she had been a widow and had a daughter from her first marriage? To try to find the answer we now consider the final daughter, Withburga, 'Stronghold of the Spirit'. Withburga was a much younger sister and would have been far less influential in Etheldreda's childhood life than the two mature examples of piety, Sethryd and Ethelburga.

We know that their mother's first husband had died – or, more probably, been killed in a conflict of 616 when King Redwald defeated all his foes only to lose a much-loved son in the final battle and then retired, weary and sad of heart, to the pastoral peace of Rendlesham. A young widow of one of the king's thanes would not have had to wait long for re-marriage and it was probably no more than a year or two later that she became the wife of Prince Anna, now in charge of the defences outside Exning.

Sometime after Etheldreda's birth Anna's wife – probably in her mid-thirties – had her daughter Withburga. It has been suggested that she died in childbirth and this seems not unlikely. (Had she been alive when Anna and Iurminus were killed in 654 she would have retired to a monastery, as was the almost invariable custom, and history would surely have recorded it.) At this time Etheldreda would still have been very young and may indeed hardly have known her mother. It would have been always Seaxburga to whom she turned in those early years, for comfort and advice.

Withburga was not a strong child and was sent to the Holkham residence on the Norfolk coast for the sake of her health. Here she seems to have initially developed into something of a recluse but she later founded a nunnery at East Dereham, becoming its first Abbess. Local sources tell us that the convent was founded on the death of her father the king in 654. As Withburga was Anna's youngest daughter she must have been in her early twenties, or even late teens, when she established this convent. Women were used to taking on burdensome responsibilities very young and Withburga clearly followed the rest of this remarkable family in her determined dedication to her beliefs, and in putting them to practical use. As the closest member of Anna's family still responsible directly to him it would have fallen on her to commemorate his death in battle by the foundation of a religious community. Her convent was among the earliest ones to have been set up in the kingdom of East Anglia, following only a few years after Bishop Felix's monasteries at Dunwich and Soham, Sigbert's abbey at Bury St Edmunds, and Anna's own foundation at Blythburgh.

Here at Dereham Withburga's body was interred. She never became Abbess of Ely; she may have had no wish to move from her own nunnery, or perhaps her death – though reputedly in old age – preceded that of her particularly long-lived elder sister, Abbess Seaxburga. Withburga was made a saint – she has been called 'the loveliest of all the Saxon saints' – and her remains became an important focus of pilgrimage. It may be significant that when the East Anglian diocese was split into two some twenty years later, a Saxon cathedral was built at North Elmham, only five miles away. Withburga's body stayed in the Dereham sanctuary until taken away in stealth by the Ely monks three hundred years later, but Withburga's Well in the churchyard is still much visited today. It is a strange quirk of circumstance that Anna's youngest daughter should have been the first to become the revered head of a religious house – the first of a truly remarkable family.

Etheldreda's youngest sister, Withburga, founded a nunnery at East Dereham, and her burial-place is perpetuated by a spring-fed well which never runs dry.

3

THE STANDARD-BEARERS

It is now time to introduce a number of notable people – people outside her own family – who would have had an influence upon the young Etheldreda. As we know, impressions received in early life are often decisive in moulding one's adult character. The natural environment into which Etheldreda was born, the varying and sometimes conflicting attitudes of members of her family and of others known to her, and finally – and crucially – the buffeting to and fro by momentous, and often terrible, events – all must have helped to persuade Etheldreda to embark upon the courses in her life through which we know her today. So let us now look at some of the men and women whose ways of life, strongly and rigidly adhered to, could well have made impressions upon Etheldreda in the days of her childhood.

An Irish monk named Fursey, apparently of royal blood, descended upon East Anglia with a few followers early in the reign of Sigbert. Fursey, a mystic, bound himself into the Celtic version of Christianity. He was convinced of the power of solitary prayer and opposed formalised religion. His method of conversion was to wander through the countryside preaching to ordinary people as and where he found them; he would then return to his remote cell to wrestle privately with the devil. This was totally alien to Sigbert's own form of Christianity, received upon his baptism in France. Sigbert's faith, taught by the Burgundian bishop Felix, belonged to the formal Roman system. But despite his fundamental differences with the Celtic form of Christianity, Sigbert – clearly a kindly and magnanimous man – welcomed the newcomer and permitted him to settle in some modest comfort within the walls of an old Roman fort at Burgh Castle in Norfolk.

So Fursey constructed his hermitage – a very basic cell – and there lived his life. When Sigbert was slain and Etheldreda's father Anna became king he in turn nurtured Fursey, enlarging and embellishing his cell. Anna gives us the impression of being both intelligent and shrewd, and his solicitous attention may have taken account of the relationship of this monk to Celtic royalty on the far side of Penda's pagan Mercia. But his showering of gifts was an embarrassment to Fursey, who duly retired to another haven. On Anna's death in battle in 654 Fursey decided to leave East Anglia altogether and go to France; there he was well received and lived out the two remaining years of his life in monastic seclusion.

Without question Fursey possessed a dominating personality. His influence on kings and their offspring would however have been limited by his austere and solitary lifestyle. Fursey would have been oblivious to the aristocracy of the times, busying himself with the ordinary people – swineherds and shepherds, tillers of the soil, tanners and weavers – encountered on his outings into the countryside and the villages and hamlets. It must be doubtful, to say the least, whether Anna would have looked with any favour at all upon his own children coming under the influence of Fursey's Celtic Christianity, which was quite alien to the one in which he himself had been – literally – immersed. But although Etheldreda may have been kept out of Fursey's way she could not have been prevented from knowing of his ideas and lifestyle.

With our second personage the tale is quite different. Shortly after Sigbert had settled down as king of East Anglia his mentor Bishop Felix arrived in Kent. The Archbishop of Canterbury sent him by sea to East Anglia where he landed at the place now called Felixstowe. Sigbert then established Felix as East Anglia's first Bishop, with his seat at Dunwich. It was here that he founded a monastery and established a young peoples' teaching centre based upon his own knowledge of monastic schools in France. There the great abbeys embraced institutions to which young women from Kent and East Anglia were sent to be educated in both religious and lay subjects, Etheldreda's two sisters going to Faremoutiers. It is highly likely that daughters of wealthy, and especially royal, parents, would have attended Felix's school.

Equally probable would have been Etheldreda's own instruction at that school. Her father had become king when she was about ten and the family would then have spent most of the time at Rendlesham; Anna would not have remained long at Exning now that the victorious Penda was away in the north. There was the important wedding of Seaxburga to the new king of Kent to be arranged and this could not be done from remote Exning. So at this critical period in Etheldreda's life between the age of ten and the marriageable age of around sixteen her education would have been under Bishop Felix at his nearby monastery. Not to have participated would have been unthinkable; young ladies of the court had to be well versed not only in the detail of Roman Christianity but also in Latin and crafts such as needlework and manuscript illumination. When Etheldreda founded her own monastery at Ely she introduced a similar school into that foundation.

Felix's influence upon Etheldreda would not, however, have been confined to his role as her tutor at Dunwich. His devout way of life and the reverence accorded to him as the first Bishop of East Anglia must certainly have made a strong and continuing impression on the young princess, as on other members of the royal family at Rendlesham. But it would have been an event of several years earlier when Etheldreda was perhaps no more than seven years old, and her father still in command of the stronghold at Exning, that planted the first seeds of her faith: the family baptism, conducted by Felix himself. Where it took place we cannot know for sure, but the firm likelihood is that the Bishop would have come over to Exning for the ceremony and also to look at a part of the kingdom which was still not wholly Christian. It may well be that he then decided to set up the monastery at Soham as a base for the preaching of the gospel. This monastery, to which Felix's bones were later transferred from Dunwich, has entirely disappeared, destroyed by the Danes in 970, but it seems to have been a large and thriving institution. Whether its foundation was triggered off by Felix's visit to the princely court can never be known but the formation of a monastery just four or five miles away is surely significant.

In this clear stream near Exning, with its healing waters, the child Etheldreda was baptised.

It is said that this family baptism took place in the little stream by the springs issuing from the copse near Exning. The ceremony, though probably not fully understood by the child Etheldreda, would have remained always in her memory as a quiet, solemn and reverent occasion and must have played its part in guiding her towards her pathway through life.

What, now, of two sisters who left their mark on the young Etheldreda in very different ways?

We come first to the widow of a battle-slain king. We have seen how Sigbert reigned over East Anglia for just a few years and then abdicated to dwell as a monk in the monastery he had himself founded, and how his cousin Egric became King. But we know that around 640 the long East Anglian peace was finally broken as the mighty Penda invaded the country – taking advantage, we must assume, of a temporary absence of Prince Anna from the defences. Egric and all his troops were massacred, and Egric's widow, Queen Hereswith, set out for the monastery at Chelles, near Paris, to retire from the world.

Etheldreda, ten years old, would have seen a ransacked, burnt-out palace at Rendlesham, with her uncle dead and beheaded, her revered cousin Sigbert slain in self-ordained martyrdom, and her aunt Hereswith gone away to forsake her country, and the world, for ever. With the awful deaths of many men of the royal court – men she would have known well and probably admired as childhood heroes – her trauma must have been intense and it is not difficult to believe that the first glimmerings of desire to become a nun like Hereswith would have entered her consciousness.

Hereswith had come down from Deira – what, roughly, is now Yorkshire – to marry Egric. Ever since Redwald had installed Edwin as King of Northumbria there had been links between that kingdom and East Anglia, and Hereswith was Edwin's great niece. But it is to her sister Hilda, born in 614, that we now turn.

Hilda is accepted as the greatest of all English abbesses. She was brought up in Northumbria in some style but decided – at probably about the time her brother-in-law was killed and her sister retired from public life – to renounce earthly pleasures and to take the veil. At the age of thirty-three Hilda resolved to join her sister and made her slow sea journey southward, taking a respite from her perilous voyage to stay at the royal court, once home to her sister and now the seat of King Anna. Etheldreda would by this time have been seventeen, so we are now at the end of her adolescence; indeed custom decreed that she was more than ready for marriage.

There had been great sadness in Northumbria when the devout Hilda left for the French monastery, and Bishop Aidan of Lindisfarne now sent a message to Anna's palace pleading with her to change her mind. Hilda herself must surely have been beset with mixed feelings about her decision to embrace a Christianity different from the Celtic form she knew and understood, and the request from Aidan was too much for her to resist. She returned to Northumbria and it was not long afterwards that she moved to Whitby, there to set up the greatest double monastery in the north.

Hilda was an inspiration to all who came into contact with her, and indeed to many who knew her only by repute. She was truly a mother figure to rulers and ruled alike. Her influence on Etheldreda, now growing into a young woman, must have been tremendous. Hilda's stay at Rendlesham was a long one, with time for many hours of conversation with the Princess. If Bishop Felix exerted the foremost male influence outside her own family there can be no doubt that Hilda was his female counterpart. But while Felix's Christianity was Roman, Hilda's beliefs would still have been basically Celtic, even though she was heading for the Benedictine monastery at Chelles. Felix himself had little time left but Hilda's great years were still ahead.

As time passed a renewed menace from the warrior king Penda became ever more apparent, King Anna having incurred Penda's wrath by giving asylum to one of his enemies. Anna would therefore have needed to spend an increasing amount of time at his frontier stronghold at Exning. Here far reaching strategic decisions had to be made and, as a result of political necessities, Etheldreda's years at home were to come to an end. But these people she had met in her childhood must have fundamentally influenced her outlook on life, and we can perhaps get some sense of their contribution towards the moulding of her personality.

4

THE CHOSEN WAY

Amid the turmoils – intrigues, treacheries, massacres, burnings – surrounding Etheldreda's young life there would have been blessed havens of tranquillity. Indeed for her first ten years she must have lived much as village children did in the days before the war, wandering alone or with Seaxburga through copses and meadows and by the stream in the idyllic atmosphere of the Exning countryside. Saxon families of standing liked to build their halls and homesteads on a slight eminence, free from risk of flooding and overlooking a source of fast flowing fresh water, or perhaps by a clear spring. As time passed and Etheldreda's family were baptised in the Exning stream, a rudimentary oratory – wooden, thatched, little more than a hutment, with an altar, sacramental relics, and ceremonial pieces within – would have been erected on the hill for family worship, by the very birthplace of the child Etheldreda.

For healthy children – and one can assume from Etheldreda's remarkable life that she had an inborn resilience, while Seaxburga's restless energy is beyond doubt – these early years must have been happy ones, partly in response to the beautifully peaceful natural surroundings and partly due to a good, Christian family life. If the mother had indeed died and Withburga, as she grew up, was not only of indifferent health but solitary by nature, it would have been Seaxburga with whom Etheldreda sought companionship. Their subsequent history, up to and after Etheldreda's death, makes the closeness of the relationship abundantly clear. And over the two children there breathed the beneficence of a truly Christian king, their father Anna.

The East Anglian kings ruled from Rendlesham near the Suffolk coast; here the great hall stood above the grassy banks of the river Deben.

But in 640, when Etheldreda was ten and Seaxburga about fourteen, their world fell apart. As we have seen, Penda invaded East Anglia and killed King Egric, ex-King Sigbert, and the flower of the kingdom's nobility. On his withdrawal he left East Anglia in utter desolation and Anna, returning to take up the kingship at Rendlesham, must have been in a state of despair. It says much for his resilience and determination, as well as his shrewd statesmanship, that within two years of his assuming the throne he had secured a firm alliance with Kent by marrying Seaxburga to King Erconbert.

The ferocious destruction of Etheldreda's peaceful world, and the departure of her devoted sister for Canterbury not long afterwards, must have instilled in her a sense of intense loneliness. At no more than twelve years old she was left with no one to turn to and her agonies of mind can hardly be imagined. With her father preoccupied with the defence of his kingdom her family life was effectively at an end. Her physical presence remained but she must have been initially very much a lost soul, open to influences from all kinds of sources. Fortunately, her father was a good and understanding man and he would have realised that despite urgent affairs of state he had a young and forlorn child to care for. His daughter was still too young to be considered for matrimony and in any case the essential alliance with Kent had already been made. So Etheldreda had to be ministered to, and one can well believe that she was sent away for long periods to study under Bishop Felix at Dunwich.

The monastery of Bishop Felix at Dunwich has long been lost to the ever-encroaching waves of the North Sea.

Etheldreda, now in her early teens, would have found herself in a situation where she could couple academic learning with long reflections on her experiences of life. For perhaps the first time she could fully recognise and understand the motivation of Sethryd and Ethelburga in preparing to go to the monastery in France. She could equally sympathise with her aunt, Hereswith, who abandoned the world for the monastery at Chelles when her husband Egric was killed. She would have been filled with horror at those of the East Anglian court who had so little respected Sigbert's sacred vows that they dragged him from his own monastery and tried to turn him from a man of peace to one of war. And she would have been led, day by day, into a fuller and deeper understanding of the way of life exemplified by her mentor, Bishop Felix, while still able to admire from afar the strength of conviction of the reclusive Irish monk Fursey at nearby Burgh Castle. And then in 647 there came that vital visit of Princess Hilda of Northumbria.

It would surely be wrong to assume that Etheldreda's traumatic childhood experience cast a long-term blight over her years of education. After her initial depth of shock at the events of 640 she would, with the healing of time, have settled down in a stimulating atmosphere under her great tutor, to question and learn. There would have been other young women of the Saxon nobility with whom she could talk, and vie in fashion. At the very close of her life she said – with contrition – that she wore jewellery and gold in her early days. And there would have been outdoor pursuits, riding in particular. Etheldreda was doubtless given the best horses, and would have become a very proficient rider.

At all events the influences were now in place, and Etheldreda took her first historically recorded decision within the climate of these influences, and the weight she attached to them. She vowed to dedicate her whole being, for the rest of her life, to the service of Christ.

Such a commitment was not unusual. Sethryd and Ethelburga would have taken the vow of celibacy in France, and Withburga would in turn take her vows on becoming a nun. Seaxburga was the exception – perhaps because her father put her marriage in place just in time. It was not abnormal for princesses to become nuns and to thereby forsake marriage; after all, their husbands would more often than not be killed in battle, leaving their royal widows to take the veil as a matter of course. Why not, therefore, avoid the whole sorry business and go straight to a convent? The genuine dedication of some young Saxon ladies has been questioned and it has been suggested that monastic life was simply a sensible and practical option. Although there were no monasteries available to women in East Anglia Etheldreda might indeed have let such broad thoughts cross her mind, but her whole history gives the lie to these being the sole reasons for her decision.

We cannot know what was going through Etheldreda's mind when she made her vow, but everything in her childhood story must have been turned over and over in her thoughts during these early years. The alternative view that she received a sudden spiritual message unconnected with anything in her earlier experience, is a perfectly valid one. But Etheldreda's subsequent life history, tied in so closely to earthly events, does not paint her as a religious mystic, or as a person immune to human emotions.

While the spiritual side of any human being is a natural secret, immune to exploration, one may look further into related matters of mundane historical fact; for, after all, this undertaking – the dedication of her whole being to Christ – was to dominate Etheldreda's life and set in train the sequence of events which culminated in the foundation of her monastery at Ely.

At any critical time in a person's life there are bound to be external human influences which affect that person's emotions. So we have looked at the whereabouts of certain people at crucial periods, and how they might have made their individual contributions to Etheldreda's thinking. Beyond this, one can only engage in historical guesswork. Of course if one takes the view that, like Joan of Arc, Etheldreda made her commitment as a result of a sudden visionary revelation, she could have taken her decision at absolutely any time in her adolescent years. But if it was arrived at, at least in part, through family background, the tragic roll of events and the influence of great religious figures, then we can perhaps get some sense of when Etheldreda's vow would have been made.

One may nevertheless persist with the belief that Etheldreda was a wholly saintly figure, living in some kind of mystical other-world which made her totally oblivious to the ordinary ebb and flow of human affairs. But surely if this had indeed been so it would have been impossible for anyone to relate to her, and no power on earth could have brought her into marriage – not just once, but twice in her lifetime. Yet, as we shall see, she was persuaded in her early twenties to marry Tonbert of Ely, and she must thereby have accepted as critical the down-to-earth reasons put forward by her father. There is absolutely nothing in Etheldreda's recorded history which could lead one to believe that she lived in a trance-like world of her own, free of human feeling herself and totally indifferent to the emotions of others. On the contrary, we know that she delighted in company and listened closely to advice, that at times she could be 'difficult', and that she shed many tears as the years rolled on.

So there are three questions, born not of motive but of fact, to which we need answers if we are to get the fullest picture of Etheldreda's life and character and, moreover, to appreciate why some within her circle regarded with disfavour, or dismissed as of no consequence, the undertaking she had made.

First, did she make a formal vow in the presence of the new Bishop of East Anglia (Felix himself had just died), or privately and in an intensely personal manner? Probably the latter. The diocesan beliefs were based on Benedictine formalism, and Etheldreda's proposed vow would have seemed highly irregular. Women would take the vow of celibacy along with their other vows, after a time as novices in a monastery, nunnery or convent. This young lady was wanting to make a promise that was quite outside the Bishop's experience and – knowing that King Anna would be unlikely to favour such a decision – he would have been very uneasy about giving it his blessing. It is, one may think, more likely that the commitment was individual and personal but this would have made it, in Etheldreda's mind, no less solemn, and her adherence to it no less justifiable.

Second, did she divulge her pathway to others? Almost certainly yes. Not to all and sundry, but doubtless to her own family and in particular her father. Since she must have expected Anna to select for her a 'useful' marriage in the fullness of time it would have been unfair to him to have remained silent. The way Etheldreda had chosen for herself implicitly excluded marriage; though her undertaking did not actually bind her to remain single there can surely be no doubt that any thoughts of marriage would have been cast from her mind as she took the vow, and it would have been pointless not to have made this clear to those concerned with her future.

Third, and finally, when was the vow taken? This question matters more than may be immediately apparent. If Etheldreda's father was already sceptical about the value of a vow which his daughter said she had made, but which had not been received through the proper ecclesiastical channels, such scepticism would have been magnified if he believed the vow was made by someone barely out of adolescence. Certainly Anna needed the marriage to Tonbert for political and strategic reasons and perhaps his conscience was eased by a down-grading of Etheldreda's vow, but it may have been that he truly doubted its validity. We should not automatically award Anna a black mark, for he had a duty to his country which – as he saw it – could only be fulfilled by the marriage of Etheldreda to Prince Tonbert.

We do not have to look far for a convincing timing; it can surely be linked with the visit of the noblewoman Hilda in 647, when Hilda was thirty-three and Etheldreda seventeen. Hilda herself was in the throes of making two agonising choices. Should she put duty to her nation before personal desire? And should she re-embrace the Celtic religion of the north or accept the Benedictine life of French Christianity? She would have welcomed beyond measure the opportunity to talk over her problems with a sensitive and well-informed young woman like Etheldreda. And the impressionable Etheldreda would have been much affected by Hilda's story of rejection of earthly wealth, her religious conflicts, and her final decision to return to a holy life in her own country. It may not be too much to say that Hilda replaced Sethryd and Ethelburga as Etheldreda's rôle model and that the younger woman became in effect a disciple, embracing all that Hilda stood for – and indeed Hilda's devotion to her sister Hereswith must have struck a personal chord with Etheldreda, who had lost her own sister–companion to Kent.

So, if neither the formality of Felix not the asceticism of Fursey fitted exactly into Etheldreda's developing religious beliefs, Hilda's compromise would have seemed an answer – indeed, throughout her life Etheldreda's religion did seem to follow that of Hilda. In Etheldreda's future life in Northumbria her dislike of pomp and ceremony smacked very much of 'Hilda-ism', as did her ultimate act of constructing a great monastery rather than seeking solitude in a rude cell, as was the Celtic way.

Therefore we may assume that upon Hilda's departure Etheldreda was prompted to emulate her in every way she could and her own spiritual nature, coupled with the sum of all those earlier influences, moved her to take a vow of dedication – the very same as Hilda herself may well have taken before leaving Northumbria, and subsequently divulged to her younger companion. Felix, the only person who might have discussed matters further with Etheldreda, had just died. And so, while the fervour was still upon her, Etheldreda made this culminating vow.

If this reasoning is correct, Etheldreda made her dedication at somewhere around seventeen years old. Such a young age, together with the unconventional way the vow was taken, perhaps allowed King Anna to convince himself that his daughter's undertaking, however genuine, was not a binding one. But Etheldreda, as we know, saw things very differently – to her a vow was made to be kept, and keep it she did through all the many stresses and strains of her future years. Of course the simple religious beliefs of that time would leave no one in any doubt that breaking a solemn vow of this nature would result in the culprit going straight to a demon-infested hell, and it cannot realistically be asserted that this would have been overlooked by Etheldreda, but it would have only added its weight to the stand her own principles had already conditioned her to take.

To tackle this period in Etheldreda's life is not the most comfortable thing in the world, but it has to be done because the promise Etheldreda then made decided her path in life until the day she died. Had she not elected to make this dedication, make it early in life, and declare it to her father the King, she would probably have been married off in her teens to some young princeling of the court, had children – perhaps against her wish – and lived out an obscure life somewhere in eastern Suffolk. An easy life, but not the one she was setting her heart upon. As it was, she became one of the most remarkable women in early English history, and gave rise to a story that ended with the creation of the great monastery from which stemmed, in direct descent, Ely's magnificent cathedral of today.

5

TONBERT'S ISLAND OF EELS

The Island of Ely

(oblique from the south)

Approximate distances from Braham
(Cratendune?)

Ovin's Church	5 miles
Ely monastery	1¹/2 miles
Soham Monastery	5¹/2 miles
Exning	11 miles

King Penda was not to be quiet for long. Anna, chivalrously but perhaps naively, had given asylum to the king of Wessex, who had married Penda's sister and subsequently abandoned her. Not unnaturally, Penda harboured resentment against Anna and was biding his time before resuming hostilities. Anna had created real trouble for himself and his kingdom because Penda, though tolerant in religious matters – he permitted Christianity to be practised in Mercia – would not put up with any family insult. And indeed Anna knew that the writing was on the wall and moved his court back to Exning to renew his defences.

We are now at mid-century and Etheldreda is twenty years old. With the others of Anna's family gone she was the only one in whom he could confide – if we leave aside the rather wooden figure of Iurminus the son. Anna would now have looked upon Etheldreda with the same regard that he had for Seaxburga. He had rightly thought Seaxburga well worthy to do a good job as the queen – and his representative – in Kent, and he must also have had respect for the views of Seaxburga's younger sister and close companion. So we can assume that Etheldreda accompanied her father to Exning and resumed her acquaintance with the pleasant countryside she had known as a child.

What, though, of her vow of dedication? Anna may have remained sceptical – this was just another whim of his idealistic daughter – but at the same time her decision might not have been wholly unwelcome to him. It ensured her presence at the court as a well-educated confidante with whom he could discuss religious and other matters, and he could deploy it to deter princely suitors.

As time passed rumours became certainties: Penda was determined on a second invasion. It was clear that in 640 Penda had got wind of a temporary absence of Anna from Exning and taken his chance to ride unopposed through the ditches. It was also painfully obvious that Anna had been totally ignorant of Penda's build-up of horse soldiers. It was now essential that East Anglia should be forewarned, and an obvious way of ensuring this would be to establish the closest possible intelligence links with the frontier island of Ely.

The territory of the South Girvii, which included this and several smaller islands, could not be expected to provide armed help. Its potential was no more than a few hundred men, few if any of them good riders such as abounded on Anna's chalk downs. Moreover Penda would not need to subdue these outlying islands; he could bypass them along the southern edge of the encompassing fens and thence sweep through the defensive dykes and across the open chalkland. But the largest island, at Ely (though the settlement of Ely itself did not then exist), was ideally placed to function as an early warning system. Spies could be recruited to thread their ways through the surrounding morasses, the reed beds, pools and streams, to pick up information along the Mercian border. So Anna saw it as vital to ensure that Ely should be bound tightly to his own kingdom. But how best to do this?

Ely was, in theory at any rate, a small vassal-state, its ruler, or Alderman, appointed by the East Anglian king. The people of the islands were a tribal group, including some vestigial Celts, with inter-marriage over the centuries between the Anglo-Saxons and the British who had sought sanctuary on this remote island when their compatriots were being driven into Wales and the southwest. Anna would have selected the most able and reliable man he could find, and created him Alderman. But basically he would have been a chieftain-farmer.

Anna would obviously appoint a head man who, even if not enthusiastically supporting East Anglia, could not be won over by Penda against that kingdom. This meant a strong and steadfast man with some evidence of Christian principles. It also required proven leadership qualities, meriting a general acceptance by the tribe – which implied most probably a person put forward by the locals themselves as someone they could trust and respect. Inevitably this could only mean a man of experience, and this in turn suggests that he would be of mature years.

This man was Tonbert – Alderman Tonbert. He can best be visualised as a middle-aged farmer. It is now the year 652 in our history and when in that year Anna decided that the time had come to seal another alliance – the alliance with Kent over again, but writ small – Tonbert may have been into his forties. He could indeed have been over fifty, but this was regarded as elderly in those days and men past their prime would probably have been supplanted – simply put out to grass – in a rough, tough community like the South Girvii. What is very difficult to credit is that Tonbert was a young princeling in the Galahad mould; a youngster would not have commanded the necessary respect. It is likely that we have painted a more realistic – if less romantic – picture of Alderman Tonbert.

Over at Rendlesham the years had passed quietly enough with Etheldreda apparently at peace with herself, teaching and counselling her unlettered father in religion, perhaps even helping with his statecraft, until the menace of Penda re-emerged in the early 650s. And now Anna, returned to his Exning stronghold, had to face a momentous decision: whether, despite Etheldreda's vow, she should be persuaded – even ordered – to marry Alderman Tonbert of Ely.

Anna was a responsible king of East Anglia; his nation's defence demanded an unbreakable family connection with Tonbert, and this could only be achieved by a marriage to Etheldreda. Anna would have seen it as his first duty, and a duty which extended to his daughter, to preserve East Anglia from destruction. So a reasonable conclusion is that Anna – in what must have been a meeting fraught with intense emotion – persuaded, or commanded, Etheldreda to marry Tonbert. One would hope and believe that the word is 'persuaded' for, if Anna had truly been the upright Christian drawn by Bede, surely he would not, whatever the circumstances, force an unhappy daughter into an unwanted marriage.

But would the marriage indeed have been so hateful to her? She had not vowed specifically to remain single, and provided that her commitment was respected by her husband and that he was a sound Christian, it could have been far from a disaster. She probably knew Alderman Tonbert well, living as she did within a few miles of his island – indeed they might have met frequently at the monastery at Soham – and got on well with him. He was, as we may believe, a great deal older than she was, but that was no impediment to the marriage – particularly as they would dwell together in a kind of father-daughter relationship in which she would be cherished and protected. So – by whatever her thought processes – she agreed to the request, but in her mind one thing was certain: in whichever direction her future might lie, her vow must forever remain unbreakable.

But how to persuade Tonbert – surely by now a confirmed bachelor, fully occupied with keeping his people's body and soul together – to introduce a sophisticated young lady into his tribe? Here Etheldreda's vow posed major difficulties. Tonbert would have been well aware – for Etheldreda would have been nothing if not honest about her intended life-style – of her rejection of physical relationship with a husband and this must have been off-putting, to say the least. Therefore the somewhat irritated King Anna must have sought ways of persuading Tonbert to accept Etheldreda purely as a sister or, in the light of the age difference, a surrogate daughter. Tonbert, a mature and highly respected leader of his people, would not have accepted the public humiliation which would have resulted from Etheldreda's vow coming to light. She herself would not have revealed it, but Tonbert would have nursed a fear that it would leak out in some way, so he would have required a guarantee of secrecy.

Thus while Tonbert might have been gratified by Etheldreda's presence on his island, both as a person he may have idealised and as a status symbol, he would have needed good practical reasons for forming an alliance with king Anna – or at least an agreement to stay benevolently neutral – in any war with Penda. For it can be certain that Tonbert's native shrewdness would soon have made him well aware that this was the whole object of Anna's exercise.

One may assume that gold and worldly goods would have meant little or nothing to the South Girvii. But perhaps there had been famine on the island, or severe pestilence causing the death of many labouring people, or even great fires through the farmsteads. In these kinds of circumstances Tonbert would have been open to offers of manpower to help with farming operations and in particular with getting in the harvest. So here Anna might have had a very telling bargaining card in his dealings with Tonbert. And as we have seen, Etheldreda's own acceptance rested firmly upon her concept of duty to her father and to her country. Duty and loyalty were in Saxon times the greatest human virtues of all, and Etheldreda's decision was true to those values.

So the wedding took place, perhaps either at Soham monastery or at the little church at Exning, but conceivably in some style over at Rendlesham, and Etheldreda went to the island of Ely and lived with Alderman Tonbert in a daughter–father relationship. There is no reason to believe this was other than successful. Etheldreda's life-style on the island would have become much more basic, but with her newly discovered belief in Hilda and that person's disavowal of earthly goods and pleasures this would not have worried her at all. Equally the rough nature of the people would have been shielded from her by the protection of Tonbert.

There can be little doubt about the genuine affection Tonbert felt for Etheldreda. Anglo-Saxon law prescribed a 'morning gift' following consummation of a marriage. Tonbert presented his bride with his 'jewel in the crown', the island on which Ely now stands, and the gift was publicly accepted in accordance with the secret arrangement between them. Thus did Etheldreda become Princess of the island of Ely.

In Etheldreda's time the island was a rural idyll of flowery meadows and great trees, with sparse and scattered hamlets and fishing-places.

But her peace was to be broken once more, and within the space of three years. In 654 the long-awaited attack from Penda came. It seems that Anna's own brother Ethelhere, who may possibly have still held to pagan beliefs, lured the king into a trap. We do not know exactly what happened, but despite any warnings that Tonbert might have given to Anna Penda again swept unhindered along the bare chalk ridge and into the heartland of East Anglia where, on a hill at Bulcamp, just across the river from Blythburgh in Suffolk, he joined with Ethelhere to destroy the king's forces, to slay both Anna and his son Iurminus, and to install Ethelhere as a puppet king.

On the hill-crest, across the river from his own church at Blythburgh, Etheldreda's father King Anna was killed in a great battle.

What was happening back on Etheldreda's island we do not know. Tonbert presumably tried to convey a warning message, but if Anna had taken his men away from the defensive ditches there was nothing more Tonbert could do. Penda's mounted troops would have swept by in an instant and be well on their way east before Tonbert could have got his few people together, and his tiny band of untrained men would have been contemptuously brushed aside. And so King Anna, that good and wise man, perished on the battlefield and was buried in his own church at Blythburgh.

This would have been a terrible blow for Etheldreda. But a second tragedy followed rapidly upon the first, for the very next year Tonbert himself died. We have surmised that he was considerably older than Etheldreda and he could quite simply have been exhausted with hard manual struggle and worries about his people living precariously from hand to mouth. His principality consisted of fen and marsh, with a few islands, of which only Ely had soils workable enough to produce good crops. And of course access remained slow and difficult, so that if pestilence or bad weather ruined a harvest starvation would not be far away, for in winter the islands would be truly isolated from the nearby higher lands. Life was never easy, and perhaps Tonbert was simply worn out.

With Tonbert gone, Etheldreda was once more left alone in her small world with her responsibilities as Princess and owner of the island of Ely. She was still only twenty-five years old. It seems that she then experienced, not surprisingly, an intense desire to retire from earthly things and to find what peace she could in her own hamlet of Cratendune, about a mile south of today's Ely. But she remained conscious of her duties to her people and asked the head of her royal household if he would administer the island. This man we know as Ovin.

Ovin (or Owen in his native Welsh) was clearly an eminent figure, and we can assume that, like Tonbert, he was mature in years. It is a strong probability that he was Tonbert's deputy, well versed in administration, and fully capable of carrying out the duties Etheldreda delegated to him. Ovin is supremely important to her story, and there will be much more to say about him.

So we leave Etheldreda at peace in her own haven and, as the years passed, developing a great and abiding feeling for what had become, in every sense, her homeland. Towards the close of her story, when she made the long and arduous journey south from the monastery at Coldingham, it was not to Exning, or Soham, or Rendlesham, or even to her sister Seaxburga in Kent, but to her own home on Ely's island, the place which meant more to her than anywhere else in her world.

The tangled marshes served the islanders well in fish and wild-fowl, but were no place for human venture.

6

CRATENDUNE AND OVIN

On the Island of Eels – as Ely's isle was known – the widowed Princess Etheldreda had been faced with the daunting prospect of looking after her estate. In the first place she had no experience of management of what may well have been a fairly unruly people. She would have done what she could to help her husband, because a sense of duty to her country was, as we have seen in the case of East Anglia, second nature to Etheldreda, and the South Girvii were now her people. But to handle the administration on her own was quite beyond her and she clearly realised this in her appointment of Ovin, the head of her household, as 'steward' of the island.

Moreover, she had suffered, in the space of two years, the loss of her father and brother, betrayed and savagely killed in battle, and then her husband whom she would have come to trust, rely upon, and – one may well believe – hold in much affection. Etheldreda, afflicted with a true sadness of heart, desired only to be at peace within Cratendune's small church, there to engage herself in daily prayer. As time passed, and the feelings of loss faded, her innate sense of duty would have rekindled her interest in the island and its people, but for a short while at least she needed to be alone and it is likely that Ovin, now governor of this and the other islands, would have transferred the administration to his own village of Haddenham.

Where exactly was Cratendune? We are told by the chronicles that it was a mile south of Ely (or rather that the Ely monastery was built a mile north of Cratendune) and that is all. The name possibly means 'Cretta's hill'; another alternative is 'hill of brushwood'.

It has been suggested on the evidence of probably pagan burials that there was early settlement on the crest of the low spine running southward from Ely to Bedwell Hey. But we know that the Saxons had a good eye for positioning a settlement, so why would they have established themselves on the very top of a ridge to which everything brought to the island's shore – iron implements, reed for thatching, wild fowl for food, livestock replenishment in hard times – would need to be dragged for at least a mile up a frequently slippery clay slope? Moreover apart from sandy water-bearing cappings at Ely and Bedwell Hey the ridge is an unkind stony clay, useable for burial siting but unsuited to primitive cultivation. These two places themselves are a long haul from the course of the river Ouse at that time. Certainly at both Exning and Rendlesham the church, which in each case we may judge to be on the site of the original clearing, stands on a hill above a stream, but these hills are very near their waterways. Anglo-Saxon settlements were typically on a low eminence as close as possible to a water source, which could be either a spring or well, or a fast flowing current where the water would be pure and good fishing always available.

A detailed study of the geology and soils of the eastern and southern shorelines, the only possible accesses at that time to Ely's island – as well as those of Stuntney island and the nearby 'mainland' in the Soham area, together with the known location of the mere at Soham and the different categories of intervening fen and marsh, suggests strongly that Etheldreda's Cratendune was situated somewhere in the vicinity of the premises of Braham Farm, with immediate access to the river and to an old Roman road now relegated to an internal island linkway. The seventh-century approach route from Exning and the Soham monastery would, one may believe, have been by way of Stuntney and the wide river which at that time flowed just below Stuntney hill; it is known that here was a fishery and landing place. From this embarkation point visitors could board a river barge and be rowed or poled the two miles upstream to the dock at Braham. Braham (possibly 'bramble ham') possessed a substantial fishery –

later owned by the monks of Ely – and there must have been adequate landing facilities there.

The majestic river wound its way through the fenland reed-beds, and here at Braham it came close enough to the island to provide an easy access from the great monastery of Soham.

This is not the place to go into detail about a number of 'outside' contenders, all of which can be shown to have major disadvantages. To cross reed beds and swamps is dangerous in the extreme, and on all sides the island was encompassed by these morasses. The wide mere at Soham, though shallow, would frequently have become extremely rough, and were one to get across it in safety there would still have been a wide stretch of waterlogged sedge and reed to traverse.

At Braham there are well-defined elevated tracts of sandy loam, and one of these may well represent the site of Cratendune. We know for certain that drinking water would have been readily available from wells sunk into the sand, which here overlies impermeable clay. Braham would broadly conform to the pattern at Exning and Rendlesham, with the advantage of access to a large, free-flowing river teeming with fish. So there is a strong option in favour of 'Cratendune' being at Braham. Although Braham was a long-settled Saxon fishing village, it may be that Etheldreda established her own sanctuary, called Cratendune, on a 'hill of brushwood' close by the fishery. From her small wooden, reed thatched church, the princess, if she so wished could have readily visited the great abbey at Soham which she knew so well from childhood. But she would, with her island safe in the hands of her steward Ovin, have spent much of her time in contemplation and devotions. None the less, it seems clear from the events of her life that she was far from being a recluse and indeed seemed positive in welcoming the company of others, so that her sanctuary would have become, as time went by, a quite active place – indeed a community, however simple, in itself.

No one can be certain of the whereabouts of Cratendune, but it may well have been here, by the ancient fishery of Braham.

We turn now to her steward Ovin. He was the 'chief minister' (as some describe him) of her 'household', and this description confirms that Etheldreda, as Tonbert's wife and as owner of the island, became responsible for a substantial and formal establishment. One can justifiably believe that Etheldreda did, as time went by, see herself as belonging – not only spiritually but certainly in human terms – to Eel Island.

As head of Etheldreda's household, Ovin would have been an experienced administrator and it may well be accepted that he was Tonbert's deputy. Probably like Tonbert he would have been a mature figure who had proved himself worthy of the respect of his fiercely independent tribe. But was Ovin a true member of that tribe? Certainly by adoption, but not necessarily by racial origin. His name is the latinised version of the Welsh 'Owen', and some romanticise Ovin as the descendant of a British people who had embraced the Celtic – then the only – form of Christianity. We may imagine that his forbears had taken refuge on the remote and perhaps uninhabited island when the Anglo-Saxons had flooded across the land several generations earlier. Ovin's ancestors would gradually have been accepted by, and intermarried with, the Saxons when they themselves settled on the island. It is indeed unlikely that there were many of these British – or Welsh – on the Ely island, since there are no British names, and all the settlements are of Saxon origin. So Ovin may have come from just one isolated family, and if this family remained staunchly Christian among the pagan newcomers it foretold the courage and steadfastness which typified Ovin throughout his long life.

Where did Ovin live? He would not necessarily have lived in Tonbert's own village – indeed were he to have been responsible for part of the island he might well have lived some way away. It has been said that the hamlet of Wentworth was named after Ovin, being originally 'Owen's Ford' and it is certainly true that old inhabitants still refer to 'Winfer' instead of Wentworth. But how did 'ford' become 'worth'? The people of Haddenham believe that Ovin was one of them, on the basis that his cross, the base of which was removed by the historian James Bentham to Ely Cathedral, was discovered at Haddenham. The top is lost, so we shall never know whether it was a

Latin, Saxon, or even a Celtic cross, but undoubtedly the dedication (we will come to this at the close of Etheldreda's story) is to Ovin.

There is a medieval reference to a fishery called Gratene in Haddenham, and the resemblance to the name Cratendune may be of significance but the connection, if any, is impossible to fathom. Fish and fowl would certainly have been taken at Aldreth, where the spur drops into the fen. At what is locally accepted as the site of the cross there is a saddle between two ridges, and there would have been access to marshland on both sides, and with a good supply of upland spring water it would have been a very suitable place for settlement.

One can reasonably assume that Ovin did live in the Saxon village of Haddenham – otherwise, why was the cross there? Of course, it could have been transported from somewhere else, but this seems pointless. Crosses were erected, usually on someone's death, either to commemorate that person or to provide a worshipping point at an entrance to his or her settlement. Since, as William the Conqueror was to find centuries later, access to the island at Aldreth was fraught with danger, it is unrealistic to believe that a seventh-century cross would have been erected for the second reason. Therefore we are left with the proposition that the cross was a memorial, possibly put up by Etheldreda herself when Ovin died.

It is said that Ovin's cross was placed towards the foot of the slope, rather than at the top where its stump was ultimately found. The soils map shows a thin line of sandy soils extending along the slopes of the island and continuing past the supposed site of the cross. Here the trees could have been easily cleared and a first route established; the land could be readily cultivated, and clean spring water flowed from the hillside. Tiny settlements would have grown up, linked by the driftway between Cratendune (and later Ely itself) and Haddenham. The present church at Haddenham is sited high in the village but Ovin would probably have built the original one lower down at the end of this lane from Cratendune. And it may not be too fanciful to suggest that when Etheldreda, years later, moved her church from Cratendune to a high point at the hill of Ely, Ovin, now a monk, emulated her by rebuilding his own church on the highest land available to him.

It is time to move away from geography and soils and back into history, and to look at one of the most perplexing decisions Etheldreda made in her lifetime – the decision to go to Northumbria to marry the young prince, Egfrid. But it is still fascinating to walk along the drove which Etheldreda herself may have trodden, as she went from Cratendune to Haddenham to see and talk to her steward, and perhaps to pray with him at a tiny timber chapel just above the vast wasteland of the fens.

7

THE LEAVING OF THE ISLAND

At this stage in her life Etheldreda could not have allowed herself to
think about becoming a nun; Soham and the other East Anglian and
Kentish monasteries were for men only, and she lacked totally the
organisation to take her from her primitive island home to one of the
great but distant monasteries near Paris. There was no point in
dwelling upon a future which did not exist. So in Etheldreda's mind
was no more than the living out of her days, not in the solitude of
Celtic asceticism, nor according to the ceremonies of Felix's Roman
Christianity, but somewhere between the two, with the earlier counsels
of her friend Hilda – now a Northumbrian abbess – to guide her.
Etheldreda was settled for life within her own secluded island
community. So what came about to take her, at the age of twenty-nine,
far away to Bamburgh in Northumbria?

In 659 the whole of England was at last enjoying a lengthy period of
peace. After the upheavals of the middle of the decade – when Anna
was killed by Penda, and when the following year Penda himself met
his death in battle at the reputed age of seventy – the whole country
was not only harmonious, but fully Christian. Anna's treacherous
brother Ethelhere was destroyed with Penda, and Etheldreda's uncle
Ethelwald was now king of East Anglia. Of Ethelwald virtually
nothing is known, and he was indeed as nothing in England's overall
history, but in Etheldreda's own story he played a crucial role. That he
was a Christian is all we really know, though some old histories give
him, albeit in vague terms, a good marking. He died after only a few
years and was succeeded by Etheldreda's cousin Aldulf, who regarded

Etheldreda so highly as to finance in large measure the building of the monastery at Ely.

It appears that Ethelwald himself had little consideration for Etheldreda's vows and her committed way of life for he now put to her, quite out of the blue, an apparently weird request. He insisted that she should travel to Northumbria for a second marriage but now, at the age of twenty-nine, to someone no older than fourteen or fifteen, the prince Egfrid. Etheldreda had certainly never met the boy, nor set foot in Northumbria.

To try to understand this strange instruction one has to look at the historical background. The villainous Ethelhere had been killed fighting beside Penda, by Oswy the king of Northumbria; clearly East Anglia, having allied herself to Penda, was not going to be in Oswy's good books. It behoved the new king, Ethelwald, to find favour with the Northumbrian ruler. Defeated in war, East Anglia was effectively a vassal state now that the battle had made Oswy the undisputed Overlord, or Bretwalda, of the English kingdoms. So to ingratiate himself with Oswy, Ethelwald was prepared to do his bidding – and foremost among Oswy's demands was that Etheldreda should marry his young son Egfrid. Therefore Ethelwald, in effect shrugging his shoulders about Etheldreda's own feelings, asked her to abandon her home, go to a foreign country, marry someone half her age and thereby presumably abjure her dedication to Christ. And this for no more than to gratify his new master; there would be no favours in return, for East Anglia had been vanquished in war and had to pay the price of defeat.

Oswy, King of Northumbria, was an exceptionally powerful ruler, and utterly ruthless in attaining his objectives. Opposition was swiftly dealt with, and Oswy was not particular as to the means; if a person had to be assassinated someone would readily be found to do the deed. Oswy would have had several reasons to lay down his terms of victory to Ethelwald; they must surely have included the wish to lay his hands on some riches. East Anglia was still a prosperous trading kingdom, with much of value from across the North Sea, and Oswy needed wealth to create the twelve monasteries which were to be his thanks to

God for the victory over Penda and his allies. Equally he had to ensure that the rising power of Mercia, under her new king Wulfhere, would be counterbalanced by an alliance of Northumbria and East Anglia, weak though the latter kingdom now was. Oswy's scheme was to bind together the two nations by a marriage between his young son and a member of East Anglia's royal family.

We are told, and can well believe, that Etheldreda first declined to leave her beloved island home. Her immediate, instinctive reaction would have been one of revulsion,and as she pursued her thoughts further in the light of her knowledge of affairs outside the island her feelings would not have changed. She was now princess and owner of the island of Ely, and not directly responsible to any East Anglian king – certainly not to one she may hardly have known. Moreover East Anglia was no longer at risk of invasion; Etheldreda may not have known much about Northumbria but she certainly knew that Penda was dead and Mercia now a Christian kingdom, with an abbey under construction at Medehamstede (now Peterborough) – a mere twenty-five miles away – and with Seaxburga's daughter Ermenilda as Mercia's queen. King Wulfhere would not go to war with East Anglia, the country of Seaxburga's birth. So duty to king and country was not a consideration.

What made her change her mind? Her acceptance of this second marriage is the most perplexing occurrence in the whole of Etheldreda's life story.

Was she influenced by another person? It seems a fair proposition, yet the candidates for consultation were few. Her father and husband were dead, as was Bishop Felix. Hilda was away in Northumbria. The only two possibilities were her manager Ovin and her sister Seaxburga. Ovin is distinctly unlikely; basically a local farmer, he would have known little of happenings beyond Eel Island. And any discussion with Ovin and his islanders would simply have resulted in support for Etheldreda's original refusal.

But Seaxburga is a different proposition altogether. By the Roman roads one could readily travel from Canterbury to Ely by way of

London and – now Christian – Essex, and Seaxburga could be with her sister in a couple of days. She had always been the trusted confidante of Etheldreda, and the younger woman would have valued Seaxburga's advice, based as it was on an intimate knowledge of English politics. Seaxburga was well in touch with Northumbria through the marriage of her husband's first cousin to Oswy, and her own daughter had married the Mercian king. She was ideally placed to provide information and, with her worldly wisdom, to proffer practical advice to Etheldreda. So it may well be that we see the hand of Seaxburga in Etheldreda's apparently perplexing change of mind.

From earliest times there was a precarious way, known only to a few, through the morass beyond the fishing-place of Aldreth. From here Etheldreda looked back at the homeland she would not see again for fourteen years.

What would have been in Seaxburga's mind that she should persuade her sister to leave her church and people and travel three hundred miles to a strange country to marry a boy of fourteen or fifteen she had never met? We can be sure that Seaxburga, as always, had Etheldreda's best interests at heart, so what could have been in her thoughts?

The answer, it seems, can only lie in one name: Hilda. Etheldreda's early dedication had stemmed from Hilda's example, and Seaxburga would have known this. She would have been only too aware of Etheldreda's lack of total fulfilment in her life at Cratendune. She knew that her sister's hope, however latent, was to become a nun and perhaps found a monastery, and that she could not do this in an East Anglian context. And Seaxburga was well aware of the tremendous respect all the English kingdoms had for Hilda, and of her ever-growing influence on the Saxon nobility. With all these considerations in her mind Seaxburga could well have thought it in Etheldreda's best interests to accept the request to make the long journey to Hilda's country with its double monasteries for both monks and nuns, and advised her accordingly. And we do know that Etheldreda was very receptive throughout her whole life to the advice of people she respected and, with Seaxburga, not only respected but dearly loved.

Whatever the precise train of events, Etheldreda would now treat her exile as an opportunity rather than a penance. She would put her whole trust in God, and have faith that the troubles and tribulations which would surely follow her final decision would in some mysterious manner bring her to true fulfilment at last.

8

Passage to the North

So it was that at the age of twenty nine Etheldreda and her chosen companions set out on a northward journey of three hundred miles to the Northumbrian court at Bamburgh. The island princess would have taken few personal possessions with her, for she had abjured fine clothes and jewelry when she retired from worldly things on the death of Tonbert four years earlier. She would have travelled with a wagon or two containing warm rugs under which to sleep, emergency victuals and perhaps some herbal remedies.

The journey would have taken a good many days, because although the old Roman roads still existed, they were in total disrepair and so heavily overgrown in places as to be barely recognisable. But, however stumblingly difficult of surface, these roads did in many districts traverse open, windswept country and were thus far preferable to the narrow Saxon-cut paths across heavy wet clays like those in parts of the Trent valley; here trails would meander within tall woodlands of ash and oak, with marauders lurking to raid and plunder those taking the risk of passing through their hideaways. However, we know that Etheldreda was accompanied by Ovin; he was strong and reliable, used to dealing with unruly people in the rough world of the fens and islands, so that she must have felt all the better for his presence. And Ovin would have selected some good men to escort the travellers, care for the animals, and hunt and forage for food.

Etheldreda's companions included women of her small community at Cratendune, utterly devoted to her. It has been suggested that her uncle, the king of East Anglia, hand-picked her companions from ladies of his court at Rendlesham, but this seems highly unlikely. Ethelwald, having unexpectedly found Etheldreda accepting the marriage, would not have pushed his luck so far as to dictate her associates, and one cannot see Etheldreda agreeing to be surrounded by strangers on her arduous journey. The only thing that would have made the long hard trek bearable would have been the presence of people who were inspired by her and who would have been heartbroken to have been left behind, for it seems that Etheldreda's nature attracted intense devotion. She was also a gregarious person. It is clear from successive episodes in her life that she was as happy in the presence of others as they were to be with her, and this did not apply only to those of her own sex. There is no reason to doubt that she had lived a contented life as Tonbert's nominal wife, and of course in her later years her history was closely involved with that of the great ecclesiastic Bishop Wilfrid.

Those travelling north had to cross the wide Humber river by ferry-boat.

In the meantime she possessed the almost dog-like loyalty of her steward Ovin. We know this if only because Ovin threw aside everything to accompany her on her journey north. Whether he was married we do not know, but whatever his status it was totally abandoned when his princess made her decision to go to Northumbria.

It is possible to make a reasonable shot at tracing her journey, since there were few options if she was to follow Roman routes. We can surmise that the party – substantial in numbers, and well-organised – assembled in Ovin's own village of Haddenham. From the fishing place of Aldreth they would have been poled across a mile of watery fenland to the long-peopled gravels of Willingham, and thence – probably by mule – to Godmanchester and the Roman roads. Gradually they would have worked their way north to the remains of the Roman town of Lincoln and then continued along Ermine Street to be ferried across the Humber and resume the land passage to York.

The wild scenery of Northumbria would have filled Etheldreda and her party with wonderment, and inspired within them an overpowering awe.

York was the one Roman city taken over by the Saxons. It had been the capital of the kingdom of Deira, but now Deira and Bernicia had come together to form the vast kingdom of Northumbria, and York was reduced to a subordinate centre under a sub-king. This sub-king was Alfrid, an intelligent and well-read young man, and son of the great High King Oswy. Etheldreda was doubtless made welcome but her party would not have been able to remain long in York, for the Northumbrian court was now at Bamburgh Castle, south of present Berwick-upon-Tweed. This would be a long and tiresome journey, but it had to be endured. When Etheldreda and her community finally reached the stormy coast of Northumbria, they must have been totally exhausted.

What did Etheldreda, Ovin and the ladies encounter when they finally arrived at Bamburgh?

Apart from the culture shock of encountering a gaunt wooden fortress perched upon a great outcrop of rock, above a dune shoreline washed by the pounding waves of the North Sea, the newcomers from the island of Ely would have been immediately confronted by a formidable array of total strangers. Foremost among them was the mighty King of Northumbria and Overlord of all the English kingdoms, the almost legendary figure of Oswy himself.

Like all strong and determined men, Oswy had grievous faults, but overall he may be considered the greatest of all the seventh-century Anglo-Saxon kings. His vanquishing of Penda and his allies was a remarkable achievement, but he was the recipient of good fortune. Heavily outnumbered by Penda's forces he had undertaken to make his infant daughter a nun should the Almighty grant him victory. As the battle raged, a great storm swelled the river Winwaed. Penda, now an old man, was killed on the field and when his troops, aghast at seeing their god-leader slain, tried to retreat they were largely drowned in the raging waters. Oswy's victory was complete, and signalled the beginning of his total dominance over all the English nations. And King Oswy, not unnaturally given the simplistic times in which he was living, thenceforward considered himself in close alliance with God.

Oswy had never been a modest man, and the outcome of this great battle doubtless increased his self-regard to over-weening proportions. But in truth his failings were many and various. His well-tried procedure was to start with bribery and coercion and, if these failed, to organise – as he had done with a sub-king a few years earlier – an efficient assassination. Oswy firmly believed in the great power of wealth, and indeed had tried and failed to buy Penda off before the battle of Winwaed. He was a schemer par excellence; the pity was that his ego was swollen still further by the good luck that accompanied his every move.

To a man like this a young, apparently vulnerable, woman like Etheldreda would have seemed an easy victim. He was well aware of her dedication of body and soul to Christ – for the East Anglian king would not have risked keeping this from his fierce Overlord – but clearly he dismissed this as a vow made merely to be broken. Oswy was about to unite – at least in political terms – the royal families of Northumbria and East Anglia against the strong Mercian king Wulfhere and once this had been concluded he would probably entirely lose interest in Etheldreda. But whatever the future, the first confrontation between these two – both, in their very different ways, utterly single-minded – must have been a heart-stopping occasion.

Alongside – or, more likely, slightly behind – this larger-than-life High King would have been his wife Eanfleda. Many years earlier she had been 'summoned', as the historians rather grandly say, from Kent to become Oswy's wife, when he became king of Northumbria as a young man. Clearly Oswy then regarded Kent as the ally he most needed. It is said that Eanfleda was a reluctant wife, but she accepted her fate, and the marriage produced six children, three boys and three girls. All made a noteworthy contribution to English history, but the one with whom we are concerned is fourteen-year-old Egfrid, now about to enter Etheldreda's story as her second husband.

9

THE LONG EXILE

The wedding was to be held in York rather than Bamburgh, because a stone-built palace in an old Roman city would be so much more impressive to Oswy's guests than a grim wooden castle by the grey North Sea. And now the ceremony took place in all its grandeur, and Etheldreda was joined with Egfrid in holy matrimony by Bishop Finan of Lindisfarne.

Having agreed to the marriage, Etheldreda was not the kind of person to let herself or her own people down and she would have duly gone along with all the pomp and circumstance. She was also prepared to save Egfrid's face by accepting, albeit spuriously, the 'morning gift' always made upon consummation of the marriage. In this case it was the fertile land around the town of Hexham. Later she was to make a present of this land to the prelate Wilfrid so that a monastery could be built there and this, as much as anything, aggravated the ever-smouldering hostility between Egfrid and Wilfrid.

What Etheldreda was in no circumstances prepared to do was abandon her dedication of body and spirit to the service of Christ. There is cast-iron evidence that she held firmly to her commitment throughout the marriage. As time passed and Wilfrid returned from the Continent Egfrid offered him land and wealth if he could persuade Etheldreda to break her vow. Wilfrid refused the bribe with contempt and in due course recounted the story to Bede, who duly inserted it into his Ecclesiastical History. Wilfrid also told Bede that Etheldreda had confirmed to him that her vows had been scrupulously kept, and historians have never doubted that this was the case.

Etheldreda had come to Northumbria in order that a divine purpose, not yet understood by her, could work itself out – so that, by some means as yet undreamed of, her commitment to Christ could be given its fullest substance. This in practice meant that she would, in some mysterious way, find herself translated into a nun in one of the great monasteries of the north of England. She relied totally on faith to achieve, in the fullness of time, the desire expressed in her youthful commitment, and it was her intention to show a passive patience through all the coming trials emerging from her life at the Northumbrian court.

Not the least of these tribulations stemmed from the character of her husband. Egfrid had had the strangest early boyhood that anyone could have been saddled with. We have to go back many years to the accession of Oswy to the kingship of Northumbria. Penda was already calling the tune, and he would permit Oswy to take the throne only if Egfrid were to dwell indefinitely at the Mercian court at Tamworth as a hostage. Oswy accepted this demand and the infant was taken from his mother's arms to the seat of the Mercian king, and there he stayed until Penda's final defeat and death. Thus he was brought up effectively as an orphan and in a heathen environment, and in confronting the mood-swings and contradictions of his later years one has to keep this disturbed childhood much in mind.

By his return home at the age of about ten one can scarcely believe that paganism had imprinted itself firmly in Egfrid's consciousness. It has been pointed out that Penda himself was not anti-Christian; indeed his own son Peada was converted on marrying one of Oswy's daughters, and a Christian mission was allowed to operate within the Mercian kingdom. So it would seem that no concerted attempt would have been made to instil pagan beliefs into the young Egfrid, and Peada may have

actually introduced the boy to Christianity, for he himself held strongly
to the faith and later founded the monastery at Medehamstede. Be all
this as it may, Penda himself was killed by the River Winwaed in 655,
and his successor Peada lost no time in returning Egfrid to
Northumbria.

*The mighty seat of Northumbrian power, Bamburgh castle, was in the seventh
century built of wood. Its dominating site meant that it was virtually attack-proof,
and a visual symbol of the strength of the northern kings.*

At his castle at Bamburgh Oswy was now the undisputed Overlord of
the English kingdoms. But Mercia in particular could not be relied
upon to remain obedient in the future, particularly as Penda's second
son, Wulfhere, who was strongly anti-Oswy, had gone into hiding.
When Peada was murdered in 656, and Wulfhere – quite innocent of
this crime – emerged to come to the throne, the need for a union with
a southern kingdom had become urgent, and Etheldreda was now the
only available princess. Seaxburga's daughter, Ermenilda of Kent,
would have been in every way preferable. She was still a teenager, and
had taken no religious vows. But unfortunately for Oswy his enemy
Wulfhere had made a pre-emptive bid, and Seaxburga and her husband

had agreed that their daughter should marry this strongly Christian ruler of Mercia. So, doubtless with some misgivings – for Etheldreda's life style would have been common knowledge – Oswy had 'sent for' the lady who lived in the rural peace of Cratendune.

The wedding was followed by long years of which we know virtually nothing. Etheldreda's years of exile are the lost period of her life, yet they amounted to more than one quarter of her total span. From the very start of her Northumbrian life Etheldreda engaged in her devotions with her own followers, just as she had done at Cratendune. As Egfrid was no more than a prince, and currently of no significance in royal affairs, there would have been little ceremonial involving his presence, and Etheldreda would surely have been left in peace.

What undoubtedly would have suffered was Egfrid's ego. Despite initial efforts to keep the nature of the relationship secret it would have been inevitable that in the roistering atmosphere of a Saxon hall the truth would emerge before long, and Egfrid would have become to a large degree a figure either of fun or of contempt. This, given the insecurity of his childhood, would have been more than he could cope with, and doubtless he found solace in ladies – or perhaps slave girls – of the court, perhaps as much to impress his thanes as to fulfil his own physical needs. His attempted bribe served only to spur on Wilfrid, who disliked and despised Egfrid, in his encouragement of Etheldreda's chosen life. Egfrid's need for female company is easy to comprehend and there is little difficulty in giving credence to a series of relationships. We know that Egfrid married again after Etheldreda had returned to Ely as a nun (this was quite legal as the first marriage was never consummated), and it is a fair assumption that the new wife, Eormenburga, had had a long-term liaison with Egfrid.

Eormenburga comes over in the chronicles as a very clear-cut personality. It seems that she was in direct line from Ethelbert, the great king of Kent who greeted Augustine in 597; anyway this was her

claim. It is highly likely that Eormenburga publicly replaced
Etheldreda in all but name when Egfrid became the sub-king of Deira
at York in 664. In that year Alfrid simply vanished from the face of the
earth, and Oswy replaced him with Egfrid. This meant Egfrid's move
down to York and the start of a fresh existence for him, with new
companions who could perhaps be persuaded to treat him with more
respect. The emergence of Eormenburga as an open presence may well
have been calculated to help boost Egfrid's position, and King Oswy,
who would have long since lost all interest in Etheldreda, doubtless
shrugged off the whole matter. There will be more to say about
Egfrid's mistress, determined, calculating, grasping and ruthless.
Egfrid was putty in her hands.

So we leave this chapter in Etheldreda's life with her nominal husband
– still seeking his true identity – now sub-king in York and under the
domination of Eormenburga, while Etheldreda remained a background
figure devoted to prayer and contemplation. She would not have felt
resentment towards Eormenburga, for she had never wished to be a
queen. But she fervently desired formally to take the veil, and we are
told that she asked her husband on many occasions to release her and
allow her to enter a monastery. For reasons to be looked at further
Egfrid would not let her go, and Etheldreda was to remain for a few
more years in what must have seemed to her a totally futureless limbo.
But in truth, as we shall see, her time was still to come.

10

ETHELDREDA'S DELIVERANCE

For these many years Etheldreda remained free to pursue her religious interests in company with her companions from Ely, including of course her faithful steward Ovin. But while this way of life was more than acceptable, it remained her dearest wish to enter a monastery and become a nun, and it is likely that in York she would have found ways of communicating with her girlhood mentor, the Abbess Hilda of Whitby (or Streaneashalch, as it then was – Whitby is the Danish name), and that meetings with this remarkable woman would have refreshed Etheldreda and given her new hope for the future. In the meantime she continued to plead intermittently with her husband, particularly when he became sub-king and took Eormenburga as his permanent mistress, that he might release her. But, as we know, her pleas went unheeded.

Why did Egfrid not allow his wife to go into a monastery? He had had little to do with her for years, and now had a strong mistress who was now one may well imagine accepted as his active consort.

The answer, perhaps, lay in his own pride. Egfrid was obsessed with proving himself publicly to be a worthy successor to his illustrious father. His troubled childhood had got him off to the worst possible start, and then the marriage, forced upon him by his father, was from the outset totally hollow. Egfrid, in his vainglorious way, may have expected Etheldreda to abandon her vow immediately they were married. If so he was speedily disabused. Etheldreda saw this vow as utterly sacred, the most solemn of spiritual commitments.

Egfrid maintained his stubborn refusal to let Etheldreda go, clinging to the vain hope that she could be persuaded to change her mind and thereby enhance his own stature within the court. He knew that his wife had confidence in Bishop Wilfrid and that she relied firmly on his counsels. And Egfrid would have now come to realise that Etheldreda, who had never shown any depth of feeling for her husband - though she would have understood his physical needs, and thereby accepted the status of Eormenburga – was aligning herself firmly with Wilfrid, and this of course was bound to infuriate him and make his agreement to her move into a monastery less and less likely. The upshot was a circular train of events, for as the situation became increasingly hopeless from Etheldreda's standpoint she turned increasingly to Wilfrid for moral support, thereby magnifying Egfrid's intransigence.

Here, then, was the impasse reached when King Oswy died in 670. Egfrid now became ruler of the whole of Northumbria, and Etheldreda probably the most reluctant queen in English history. She had been princess for five years and sub-queen for six; she was to be queen for just two years, and spent the whole of that time doing her utmost to renounce the throne.

For once Etheldreda had become a full queen her whole situation changed. Her husband was no longer a princeling, or even a sub-king, but successor to perhaps the greatest ruler of the seventh century. Oswy had been a remarkable and truly memorable king, quick to anger and cruel when it suited him, but preferring to cajole rather than fight wherever possible and, unlike Penda, averse to violence for its own sake. By the end of his long reign he had become a genuinely God-fearing king, and the excesses of his early years – even including murder – have in consequence been rather minimised by history. Oswy's end was a sad – almost pitiful – one. He desperately wanted to make a journey to Rome, where he could touch the most holy relics and make atonement for the sins of which he was now all too well aware. He asked Bishop Wilfrid to take him there, but the journey would have been a long and dangerous one, and the old king could not have survived it. So he died in his own palace at Bamburgh in the presence of Wilfrid, respected – with all his frailties – as a great Saxon king.

To step into Oswy's shoes was nigh impossible, and Egfrid could hardly have been less suited to the role. But he had to have a shot at it, and in his mind Etheldreda was the key to his success or failure. Eormenburga was all very well as the consort of a sub-king in York, but there were now other kings in Mercia, Kent, East Anglia and elsewhere to impress, and Eormenburga would have to be discarded, at least for the time being. East Anglia's Ethelwald had died; that nation now had a strong young king named Aldulf, who was Etheldreda's first cousin, and he would not take kindly to her being – as he would have seen it – slighted in favour of a self-seeking courtier.

Egfrid was not blessed with a high degree of insight, but he could see that the English kings were unlikely to be impressed by Eormenburga, and in what must have been a meeting crackling with electricity he now put her to one side. While the doubtless fuming Eormenburga remained side-lined, Etheldreda was introduced into the centre of palace affairs. However reluctant she was, Etheldreda was not a rebel by nature, and she duly obeyed her husband's commands in taking up a more visible role. Now in her late thirties she had, one senses, lost the sparkiness of her earlier days, and was now a gentle, even docile, person.

But ceremonial grandeur contradicted totally her chosen way of quiet study and contemplation, and the new lifestyle was something she simply could not cope with. So from the occasional meeting with Egfrid, with perhaps no more than a half-hearted request for release which she would have realised was doomed to failure, Etheldreda was now in daily tearful pleading with her husband, and after several months had gone by in this fashion he acceded to her wish.

Egfrid's decision is yet another baffling event in Etheldreda's story. We know that his change of mind was a temporary one, and that he reverted in no more than a year to his original stance. By then, of course, it was too late; Etheldreda had taken her opportunity and gone to the monastery at Coldingham, on what is now St Abbs Head.

The young king may have simply lost patience and dismissed Etheldreda in a fit of anger, but such lapses are usually short-lived, and as it would have taken Etheldreda some days to get her people together – for she did not go to the monastery alone – her husband would have had plenty of time to calm down and rescind his permission. So a sudden burst of intemperance is an unlikely explanation. Perhaps it was a gradual erosion of Egfrid's resistance, for Etheldreda's incessant woeful pleading must have been very hard on his nerves, and made him thoroughly weary. But he had dismissed Eormenburga, and could not have contemplated with equanimity the reversal, in such a short space of time, of his decision to bring Etheldreda into prominence. Appearing weak and indecisive was something Egfrid could never endure, so his every instinct would have been to stick to his guns. Yet he allowed Etheldreda to leave the court and enter a monastery. How could this have come about?

There is a possible solution. Egfrid had a chronic inability to make decisions on his own – always he sought the advice of others. This counsel was sometimes good, but it was on these occasions that Egfrid perversely ignored it – indeed its rejection led, many years later, to his death in battle in a Scottish glen. Perhaps because of his confused childhood Egfrid was uncertain of himself throughout his life. And as Etheldreda's continuing pleas were seen by her husband as increasingly tiresome, he may well have turned to someone he knew to be a strong and positive person, and that person would quite certainly have been the spurned Eormenburga. With his wife desperate to escape, Egfrid must have felt alone and quite helpless, and in these circumstances it would have been natural for him to talk to the one person who could get him to pull himself together and put him back on an even keel.

Eormenburga, of course, would have wanted nothing better than to be recalled as counsellor. Clearly her aim would be to reinstate herself

as consort – and in effect as queen – and her proposals would have
been directed to this undivided end. It takes little imagination to
speculate on Eormenburga's advice. 'Your wife [she would say] is a
religious fanatic, who will never be of any use to you physically,
mentally or in any practical way. To persevere with her is doubly
profitless now that you have the responsibilities of a king. I,
Eormenburga, was fully accepted as your partner in York, and I will
ensure that the same thing happens here in Bamburgh. Let Etheldreda
go to Coldingham, and together we will run the nation in the way your
father would have wished. In fact, Egfrid [she would have continued],
we can marry without impediment, because my contacts have told me
so. As you may or may not know, I'm not without influence in the
court.'

With arguments of this nature Eormenburga, at once determined
and wily, could well have persuaded the vacillating Egfrid to allow
Etheldreda to leave Bamburgh for ever and take the veil. The true
course of events we shall of course never know, but the foregoing
scenario would indeed explain Egfrid's remarkable turnabout.

No one can let the actions of the steely Eormenburga lead to
admiration for her for, like Oswy, she had a mind that directed itself all
too often to bad, and especially selfish, deeds. But she is a character
who is flesh and blood and we can, so to speak, love to hate her as the
villainess par excellence of the seventh century.

We are told by the monk Thomas of Ely, writing many centuries later,
that Etheldreda, while she was Northumbria's queen, wrought with her
own hands a stole and maniple, rich with gold and precious stones, for
her friend Cuthbert, now prior at Lindisfarne. There is an oddity about
this in that neither Etheldreda nor Cuthbert had any time for fine
vestments. Although the Roman form of Christianity, as exemplified
by Bishop Wilfrid, had officially prevailed, the old Celtic life-style
persisted strongly – indeed Cuthbert later renounced the monastery of
Lindisfarne and retired as a hermit to the barren Farne islands.
Etheldreda was on the same wave-length as Cuthbert, and must have

revered him. But, now that her own vanities of youth had long passed away, why should she have set her hand to designing and laboriously fashioning the kind of vestments which Cuthbert abhorred?

The answer lies, perhaps, in her state of mind at that time. She must have been in a physical and even mental exhaustion leading to fears among her companions that a total collapse might ensue – for matters, it seemed, could only get worse. Therefore, they may have reasoned, something must be done to divert Etheldreda's mind, and give her faith a chance to rekindle itself. Her old Ely friends would have been well aware of Etheldreda's artistic creativity as a young woman, her continuing love of beautiful things – even though she had abjured them herself – and her capability and patience as a needlewoman. They also knew of her great regard for Prior Cuthbert. So it may not be too fanciful to believe that it was these companions who prevailed upon their beloved mistress to involve herself in a labour of love which would bring her the quietness of mind she so desperately needed at that time.

From time to time in this story of Etheldreda's life, passing references have been made to the great prelate Wilfrid. Partly through his own magnetic personality, partly through force of circumstances, Wilfrid had taken over from Ovin the role of Etheldreda's most valued counsellor, and we now lay out the bare bones of this remarkable man's history.

Wilfrid was born in 634 – four years after Etheldreda – in one of the Northumbrian palaces, and educated by the monks of Lindisfarne. At an early age he made the long, difficult and dangerous journey to Rome, receiving the tonsure in France during his return. Back in England, he became very friendly with Alfrid, sub-king of Deira at York, and Alfrid gave him land at Ripon to build a monastery. As Abbot of Ripon, Wilfrid became a highly influential figure in northern circles, and his prestige was increased further when his oratory swayed the Synod of Whitby in favour of the Roman, as opposed to the Celtic, style of Christianity. His link with Alfrid was thereby strengthened, but he did not endear himself to Abbess Hilda, who deplored his extravagant mode of dress and lifestyle. Throughout their two lives this animosity persisted and Etheldreda, who admired and respected them both, must have frequently found herself in a quandary.

Alfrid asked Wilfrid to visit Rome again to be consecrated as Bishop of York, but on the return journey Wilfrid remained interminably in France, finally being ordained there in a splendid ceremony. On his return to England he found that his great friend Alfrid had gone missing, and that Egfrid had now become the sub-king at York. To compound his anguish, he was barred by King Oswy from becoming Bishop of York and had to return to Ripon. But shortly afterwards the new Archbishop of Canterbury over-ruled Oswy; Wilfrid now became Bishop of York, and when Oswy died soon afterwards and Egfrid ruled the kingdom, Wilfrid's wealth and influence were at their zenith.

Etheldreda knew Wilfrid from their time together at York when she was sub-queen there, and Wilfrid's counsels grew steadily more important in her life so that, as Queen of Northumbria, she found herself in an ever-increasing dependency upon his advice. That advice was in total opposition to that of the king and a kind of rivalry emerged, with Etheldreda as a shuttle-cock between them.

This then was the position when Etheldreda, supported to the hilt by Wilfrid, left Egfrid's palace at Bamburgh to take up residence in the monastery on the bleak clifftop at Coldingham.

11

COLDINGHAM ABBEY

Now that Egfrid, for whatever reason, had agreed to the departure of his wife - or more accurately his nominal wife – for the monastery at Coldingham, Etheldreda lost no time, for there was always the possibility that this king, ever uncertain in his attitudes, would change his mind. She gathered together the ladies who prayed with her in seclusion in a cell within the palace walls – few in number but utterly devoted to her – and made her way to the bleak edifice situated on the cliff top now called St Abbs – or Ebba's – Head and there she offered herself and her followers as novices to the Abbess, Oswy's sister Ebba.

The abbey was no more than thirty miles northwards along the coast. The strong salt winds which reign in this part of England would have precluded dense tree-growth, and there was undoubtedly some kind of worn pathway across the thin soil. We can safely assume this, since a year or so later no less a personage than Wilfrid, now Bishop of York, followed the same route to the abbey, where he consecrated Etheldreda as a nun, and Wilfrid was not the kind of person to hack his way through tangles of thorn-bush.

At all events Etheldreda reached Coldingham without interception. The journey would not have been a long one, probably no more than two or three days. As the little party progressed, mounted on horses or donkeys, members of the peasantry would have emerged from their hutments to offer them food and shelter. Though they would not have known who she was, they would have sensed that Etheldreda was of high birth and been ready and willing to provide guides along the various tracks to Coldingham.

And so the Abbess Ebba enters our story. What kind of person was she? Ebba was the sister of the great King Oswy, and thus aunt to Egfrid. She apparently lived to a great age, but towards the close of her life and long after Etheldreda had come and gone, she evidently lost control of her charges and there was much abuse of religious discipline within the abbey. The monastery was a 'double' one, housing both monks and nuns. They prayed and perhaps chanted together, but were otherwise strictly segregated. Such was the rule, but with Ebba's advancing years this segregation was often honoured only in the breach; moreover, the monks and nuns dressed in rich clothes and ate the wrong kind of foods. Therefore, we are told, divine wrath descended upon the monastery; after Ebba's death there was a great fire, and devotion and dignity was subsequently restored to her foundation. But this was a long time hence and there is no reason to believe that Ebba was less than thorough in her running of Coldingham at the time of Etheldreda's arrival.

Ebba's monastery was sited in a truly terrifying position on a bare windswept cliff-top.

But one is led to consider why it was that Etheldreda chose to go to Coldingham rather than to her own long time friend, the very human and understanding Abbess Hilda at Whitby. Hilda was closer in age to Etheldreda, and had a clear appreciation of the younger woman's dilemmas; moreover she enjoyed enormous prestige among all sections of the community. And Etheldreda had originally acceded to her uncle's wish that she go to Northumbria almost certainly in the hope that fate might give her the opportunity, at some time unknown, to meet Hilda and perhaps enter the abbey at Whitby. (She may not then have known about Coldingham – indeed it may not have even been founded at that time.)

There are two conceivable reasons. The first is simply relative distances. Hilda was too far away for Etheldreda, accompanied only by a few unprotected ladies, to tackle the potentially hazardous passage. In addition a long journey would give more time for Egfrid to change his mind, and perhaps ride out to kidnap Etheldreda and bring her back to Bamburgh. (We should not forget that he attempted this very thing a year later.)

There is another possibility. Etheldreda may have thought that Ebba, because of her relationship with the new king, would have had more influence with him than Hilda could have had. But this, though it is the reason commonly given, does not ring very true. Hilda was far more powerful than Ebba could ever be, and no one – certainly not Egfrid – could have defied her, whereas Ebba was no more than an aunt whom Egfrid might well have taken a perverse pleasure in crossing – as indeed he did the following year.

Etheldreda, with her companions, was now at Coldingham Abbey. The monastery, situated above a beetling cliff, was secluded to the utmost degree, totally cut off from the outside world, and from Etheldreda's point of view an ideal place in which to pursue her devotions and prepare herself to become a nun.

Etheldreda herself must have been in a state of extreme elation. At last she could formally prepare herself to receive the veil, and thereby achieve her lifetime goal. Never, since her first retirement to the small church at Cratendune on Tonbert's death, could she have been, as now, free of tension, able to concentrate fully on prayer and contemplation. At any time during her stay at York and Bamburgh she could have been summoned to participate in one or another piece of ceremonial. It is clear from Egfrid's reiterated refusal to allow her to enter a monastery that he had not been prepared to take her attitude seriously enough to defer to her wishes, for peace and quiet, though even he must have known that those wishes stemmed from a single-minded devotion to a Christian way of living. But now, at the age of forty-two, she found herself for the first time in her life within the walls of a monastery, and safe at last from the whims of her unstable husband.

Or so she thought at the time, but she could not then foresee the future, or forecast the course of Egfrid's unpredictable changes of mood. As far as Etheldreda was concerned, she would expect to become a nun within a few months, and then – if her thoughts took her that far – succeed the ageing Ebba, in the fullness of time, as Abbess of Coldingham. And indeed the first part of this programme came to pass as, smoothly and without interruption, Etheldreda and her companions took their vows under the administration of Bishop Wilfrid.

In our story of this outstanding event in Etheldreda's life we have not mentioned her erstwhile steward, and now companion in exile, Ovin. Ovin was now getting on in years. He had always been utterly devoted to Etheldreda, and her lifestyle had communicated itself to him in no uncertain way, so that he himself had for some time felt a desire to become a monk. This great yearning for the devotional peace of a monk's life in his old age brought Ovin to a decision to leave Bamburgh at the same time as Etheldreda went to Coldingham. He duly presented himself outside the gate of the monastery at Lastingham in what is now Yorkshire, armed only with an axe and a billhook, and asked to be taken in as a labourer and as a novice.

Ovin seems to have been a strange, naturally withdrawn person.

Clearly he did not see himself as a scholar, and this reinforces the view that, like Tonbert, he was basically a simple farmer, a herdsman, a hewer of wood and tiller of the fields. His life seems to have been that of a loner and wanderer in the Celtic tradition, for we hear nothing of a wife and family.

The humble Ovin was indeed admitted to Lastingham, and there became a trusted companion of the great Bishop Chad, accompanying him shortly afterwards to the Mercian monastery at Lichfield. Before long Chad had died, and it seems that Ovin was on the move once more. We do not know where he went but he did reappear in his own village of Haddenham, on the island of Ely, at the close of his life – at least we can assume this from the cross erected to him in that village. Did he go from Lichfield to Coldingham? We would like to think so and, given Ovin's capacity for hard and rigorous travel, and Etheldreda's presence at the abbey, it is more than likely that this is where his wanderings would have taken him.

But at this stage let us leave Ovin and his perambulations, and turn to perhaps the most traumatic phase in Etheldreda's remarkably eventful life.

12

ETHELDREDA IN DANGER

It appears from the chronicles that Egfrid became morose during the months following Etheldreda's departure, and the reason given is simply that he loved her deeply and could not bear the separation. Such an explanation is, on the face of it, difficult to credit. We must come to grips with a single question: could a man have any heartfelt love for a woman who had not wanted to marry him, would have no intimately physical relationship with him, pleaded incessantly to be allowed to leave him for ever, and had taken as her counsellor his greatest rival and enemy? Such a man would have to be a far more saintly figure than Egfrid.

Left without his queen, it is more likely that the king's driving obsessions would have been his almost insane jealousy of Wilfrid (culminating years later in the latter's committal to gaol in defiance of the Pope) and resentment at the loss of face her absence had now brought him. Add to that his apparently infinite capacity for self-deception, and his readiness to be cajoled by others into taking rash and foolhardy decisions, and we can make a reasonable initial guess at the reasons for his change of mind.

It is not difficult to understand Egfrid's resentment. Throughout Etheldreda's life story there are few, if any, absolute rights and wrongs. Everyone involved has his or her point of view. Let us look at this situation through Egfrid's eyes.

As a boy he had been forced into marriage with a woman twice his age, and one thought of not for her ability to make a good consort in the years to come, but for her extreme piety, expressed in her withdrawal from the real world. On marrying her he had tried to get her to love him physically, even to the extent of offering money and land to Wilfrid if the latter could talk Etheldreda into breaking her vow. For years Egfrid had refused her pleas to be released, in the delusion that this vow remained a fragile one and that in due course his own personality would be strong enough to shatter it. In other words, it had become to him a battle of wills. Later, when it became clear that Etheldreda regarded a dedication of body and soul to Christ as a serious matter, Egfrid's refusal may indeed have been motivated in large measure by spite – a reaction that can be understood, if not regarded as acceptable. Now, in a moment of weakness, prompted by pressure from the determinedly single-minded Eormenburga, Egfrid had permitted her to leave. He hated himself, and hated the world, and wanted only to be left alone.

But this theory, however plausible, nevertheless does fly in the face of the very definite historical statements that Egfrid had a profound love for his wife which he retained through thick and thin. How could this possibly have been the case?

In reflecting on this we may envisage Etheldreda not as the stubborn, cold, remote, and frankly unlovable religious fanatic to whom Victorian historians are so committed, but as someone soft in nature. Let us think of her additionally as rather immature, unsure of herself, and with the kind of vulnerability irresistible to the most hard-hearted of men. Surely, in such a case Egfrid, even though his volatility would have led him into the kind of attitudes described in the earlier paragraphs, could have also felt – at least on some occasions – strongly protective towards this emotional and indeed often tearful person, and one can imagine this extending into something which could be defined as affection, even though coupled with a fierce possessiveness and overlain from time to time by resentment and indeed anger.

Perhaps we have spent overmuch time looking at the attitudes of Etheldreda's husband, but he was after all married to her for thirteen years and cannot just be dismissed with shallow words and phrases.

And if the foregoing passages about Egfrid seem in some degree confusing and indeed contradictory, they do no more than mirror the complications of his character, with its inadequacies and insecurities, and an underlying yearning to be respected like the great Bretwalda Oswy, his father.

But to return to the narrative. Even though his nobles would have been well aware of the relationship – or non-relationship – with his wife and accepted, however reluctantly, her supplanting by the upstart Eormenburga, Etheldreda's actual physical departure from Bamburgh would have removed the last vestiges of prestige from Egfrid and rendered him something of a laughing stock within the court. The king, brought up in childhood and boyhood in subservience to others, and in manhood petulantly determined to be admired like his father, would have been quite unable to face this. Even the ministrations of his mistress could not cancel out his disgrace and one can well imagine and appreciate his chagrin, culminating in a morose and surly withdrawal from palace life. And as far as Etheldreda was concerned, his intermittent bouts of protective affection, lessening as the barren years had passed, would have drained away altogether with her absence from the court, leaving him with an overwhelming feeling of self-pitying failure.

If Eormenburga had indeed become the true – if highly unpopular – ruler of Northumbria, she may well have been not entirely unhappy with the way things were going. The high-born members of the court would not want a king who failed to govern. Egfrid would have presented no fears to them as his father had done and we can easily picture the thanes issuing an ultimatum to the king: get rid of Eormenburga, fetch your wife back, and resume at least a semblance of dignified rule – or make way for someone else. Or perhaps Egfrid pulled himself together at last, overrode the protests of Eormenburga, and came to the same decision: to retrieve, by hook or by crook, Etheldreda from the monastery at Coldingham. The second alternative seems the less likely but for whatever reason Egfrid ultimately roused himself from his torpor and gathered together a mounted party to ride to the abbey and collect Etheldreda – by force if necessary – and bring her back to the palace at Bamburgh.

Below the abbey the waves crashed unceasingly against the craggy coast of Northumbria.

While Etheldreda would have been totally wrong in assuming Egfrid would be in any way respectful of his aunt's feelings, she would have been right to assume that Ebba would be in much closer touch with the royal court than would Hilda down at Whitby. At all events Ebba got wind of what was afoot and lost no time in telling Etheldreda and advising her to escape quickly from the monastery.

Etheldreda could of course have simply surrendered to Egfrid, but she had not achieved her lifetime ambition merely to throw it away – and in any case as a nun she presumably no longer considered herself married to the king. So she immediately made preparations for a speedy departure from the monastery.

What might have happened if Ebba had asked Etheldreda to remain and give herself up meekly to Egfrid? Etheldreda would have had no alternative but to comply, for without the cooperation of the Abbess it would have been impossible to organise an escape. So Egfrid would have arrived, collected her, and returned her to the palace as queen, presumably simply refusing to recognise the veil. Etheldreda would have lived out the rest of her life in the deepest unhappiness, and there would have been neither monastery nor subsequent cathedral at Ely. All this hung on the choice Ebba had to make between her own flesh and blood and the newly veiled nun under her care.

In fact it is most unlikely that Ebba had any doubts about what she should do. She would have been well aware of Etheldreda's anguishes at having to put on a performance as a Northumbrian queen – indeed, this is why she had been welcomed to the abbey a year earlier. Now she was Ebba's responsibility; a nun in her own right. She had renounced her marriage, her queenship, and the world, and to Ebba no less than to Etheldreda what had taken place was totally irrevocable. Nevertheless we must extend much credit to Ebba for having the great courage not only to make the decision on Etheldreda's behalf but of being prepared to face up to her nephew when he arrived to find that his wife – as he presumably still regarded her – had vanished.

For she had to vanish completely to be safe from Egfrid and his fierce horsemen. Where would she go, and with whom would she travel?

Etheldreda had brought a number of her kindred spirits with her when she first came to Bamburgh. Some may have died or departed, but she would have attracted others. So it would have been a fair-sized community of deeply religious women that had made the journey to Coldingham a year earlier, fervently desiring to join their revered lady in becoming novices under Ebba. Many would have wanted to go with her now, in this time of trial. But travelling surreptitiously along secret pathways meant that Etheldreda could not possibly take a large group of these nuns, and in any case they were no longer responsible to her but to the Abbess.

It was therefore inevitable, from both disciplinary and practical standpoints, that Ebba would have limited her women companions; there were just two, named as Sewara and Sewenna. They were certainly nuns and Etheldreda may have selected them because they were originally from her Cratendune settlement, and therefore among her oldest friends.

Is it possible that three ladies would have set out unprotected on this epic journey of three hundred miles? The first stage of the journey would be the most dangerous, as they would have been at risk of apprehension by Egfrid and his men. Since they had to travel in disguise, probably as pilgrims, they would not have enjoyed the immunity from molestation that the habit of a nun would have extended to them, and there was a risk, not only of armed robbery – though they would not have had much worth taking – but also of suffering personal indignities. More than that: although Etheldreda was country born and bred she could hardly be expected to be proficient in hunting deer, trapping birds, or taking fish. But the journey was likely to be a long and arduous one, and they could not survive without basic sources of food, so it seems obvious that they would need to take with them a strong and seasoned countryman, well versed in foraging for game and in the ways of a fisherman. And here we cannot help thinking of Etheldreda's old steward Ovin.

There are few certainties in seventh-century history and it is always necessary to look at the balance of probabilities. It is very likely that when his friend Chad died at Lichfield, Ovin the great wanderer decided to move elsewhere, and we have already conjectured that his destination was the double monastery at Coldingham, the place where the person to whom he remained utterly devoted had been consecrated as a nun. He himself was either already a monk or well on the way to becoming one, and as a great friend of the much lamented Bishop Chad he could expect a warm welcome from the Abbess Ebba.

(We have to remember that Ebba, like Chad, had been raised in the Celtic tradition and, even though the Synod of Whitby had come down in favour of the Roman system, the old beliefs were still strongly held to in the northernmost parts of England.)

So should we not envisage Ovin coming to Coldingham while Etheldreda was there? And from this it is only a small step to believing that he, Ovin, would have volunteered, or been asked by Etheldreda, to accompany the three disguised nuns on their long, and in many ways fearful, journey south.

13

A MIRACULOUS JOURNEY

We can picture Etheldreda and her two companions, guarded by the hugely reliable Ovin, getting a few chattels together and setting out, mounted on horse or mule, along the rocky cliff top trackways, trying to put distance between them and the pursuers they knew would soon be starting out from the abbey. But whence were they heading?

Their first objective would be to reach the Humber ferry unseen by Egfrid and his men. Once well south of the great river they could expect to have a little breathing space in which to make a final decision on where to go. In theory there were many alternatives. In now Christian Mercia, ruled by Wulfhere and his queen, Etheldreda's niece Ermenilda, there were places where they would be safe; Medehamstede was just one of these. There was Withburga's nunnery at Dereham, monasteries at Dunwich, Bury St Edmunds and elsewhere, Seaxburga's own abbey at Sheppey – an extensive choice.

But there was one piece of land to which Etheldreda had always remained loyal, the dowry from Tonbert on which she had already founded a small church and worshipped for some four years before leaving for Northumbria: her own island of Ely. And that is where she intended to go. It would not have been a difficult decision – barely a decision at all in Etheldreda's eyes – and one can be virtually certain that she made it even before she left Coldingham. If Ovin was leading her tiny group then it becomes even more explicable, for the island was his own true homeland as much as Etheldreda's and that of her two ladies. Truly the decision would have been a simple one, and the thought of going back home would have been exhilarating, serving to spur the little party on though all the rigours and dangers of the journey. Ovin had lived not only at Ely but also in both Yorkshire and Mercia, and thus had a broad experience of travelling through varied kinds of country.

Let us now leave Etheldreda on the pathway south across the headlands, and return to Ebba's monastery, where Egfrid, more or less a prisoner of his mounted retainers, arrived to find that the bird had flown. Left to Egfrid that would probably have been the end of it. The briefest sober contemplation would have convinced him that to kidnap a consecrated nun and expect her to abandon her sacred vows and resume the life of a queen was scaling the very heights of fantasy. Far better for him to return and make the best of Eormenburga who, however ruthless in her ambition, was the most positive of women; she would certainly boost his confidence, and would not let him down. Dominant she might be, but she would provide a support against his surly thanes, and if he could convince the royal household that he had done all he could matters might yet go his way.

But it appears that the hunting instincts of his riders were well and truly up, and willingly or otherwise, Egfrid had to find the trail and follow it. However, the signs would not be easy to trace. Land of this nature was only sparsely treed, and Etheldreda's party could have made fair speed without leaving much in the way of evidence.

It may be that Etheldreda's warning of the king's intention had been very brief. This is the more likely if there had been an insidious working on his blackly morose mood by members of his entourage, followed by a sudden persuasion, perhaps when Egfrid was in his cups, that it was time to make a move. The persuasion may in fact have been more of a threat, but the important thing was to get Egfrid on his way before he could have another of his infamous mood-changes. So the 'mole' wanting to get news to Ebba would have had to move fast, and if we are to applaud Etheldreda for fleeing the abbey, and Ebba for her presence of mind at a critical juncture, we must also salute the unknown messenger who carried the news in time for an escape to be hurriedly organised.

So the pursuit was on. And from here on there ensued, we are told, a series of miraculous happenings, the first of which satisfied Egfrid that the chase must be abandoned.

There would have been no time for the party to get very far, and Egfrid's horsemen could easily outpace Ovin and the three women. So it appears that the fugitives repaired to a spur of rock linked only to the mainland by a narrow neck of sand, presumably sea-covered at high tide. Their reasoning is not clear, because in the bracing winds of the northeast the women would surely have frozen during the night. However that is what is relayed by the chronicles. What then happened was that Egfrid and his men duly caught up with the tiny party perched upon their rock, and glared balefully at them while they waited for the tide to ebb. However, so the narrative continues, the sea became ever more fierce and, far from receding, built up into a crescendo of sound and fury, terrifying the thanes and leading Egfrid to believe that the Almighty was taking the same kind of hand as had been evident to his father Oswy. A burning of Bamburgh had been arrested by a sudden change of wind, and Penda's army had been finally defeated largely because of a sudden flash flood. Egfrid would have had these events drilled into him in his early years, and would have been fearful that the elements were now conspiring once again. This concern would have been communicated to his horsemen, and they now backed away and returned to Bamburgh. But once Egfrid's superstitions had passed there can be little doubt that he would have regarded the event as working for rather than against him, for he could now bring his warriors back to the palace with the story that a miracle had intervened to save the hunted party, and that he could not be expected to compete with divine providence.

And that is exactly what Egfrid did. He straightway returned to his court, where he presumably had first to soothe the furious Eormenburga and then, honour satisfied as far as his nobles were concerned, started a new and more dignified life with Eormenburga shortly to become his legal queen. It appears that he was free in the eyes of the Church to remarry now that Etheldreda had taken the veil.

We might ask what would have been Etheldreda's status had the kidnap been successful. But clearly the outcome, however achieved, was the best for all concerned.

The story as chronicled could have a basis of fact. There might indeed have been a storm. But one wonders how Etheldreda and the others could possibly have survived, even though they could presumably have found a kind of burrow in the rock. Moreover Egfrid was a coastline man, and he would know that this kind of upheaval can die away within hours. However if he suspected a supernatural occurrence, or, more prosaically, if he was looking for an excuse to retire with honour, then even a short-lived storm could have sufficed. While the narrative does have elements of extreme unreality about it, there must have been some happening that would convince not only a half-hearted Egfrid, but also his quite determined companions, that they would have to go home. It has been suggested that there was a sudden surge of water across his route – perhaps a repeat of the sort of flash-flood which occurred at Winwaed – brought about by a fearsome thunderstorm which soaked his party to the skin. Bedraggled, their way frighteningly barred, their spirits would have been lowered to a point where they would have wanted nothing more than to return to Bamburgh and get some good ale inside them. During a rueful retreat they might well have concocted this story of a miracle, and faces would thereby have been saved.

Whatever happened, Etheldreda and her party were free to venture on, but of course they would not have realised that Egfrid had given up, and would have continued their journey still in the belief that they risked being captured.

It is at this point that we must say farewell to Egfrid, an utterly mixed-up man and just about the worst possible match that could have been chosen for Etheldreda. His future was to be no better than his past. Eormenburga gave him a terrible time, totally dominating him and getting him to do things alien to his better nature. Years later, for example, he cast Wilfrid into prison in outright defiance of the Pope;

Eormenburga had conceived a great hatred for Wilfrid, who had castigated her roundly for her wrong-doings, and she took to wearing his sacred relics as a necklace. As a result she developed fits and only recovered on the release of the Bishop.

In later years Egfrid followed his father in paying more attention to religious matters, but he remained supremely erratic. After a foolish invasion of Ireland he ignored wiser counsels and attacked the Picts, leading his men into a remote glen where they were duly ambushed and perished to a man. Thereupon Eormenburga the so-called 'she-wolf' decided to take the veil, and in due course became probably the most unlikely abbess in English or any other history.

We return to Etheldreda and her companions. Travelling clandestinely but with all the speed they could muster, in due time they reached the mile-wide Humber and were ferried across it to the northern end of the Roman Ermine Street. But at this stage for a while they would have had to be particularly wary, for the traverse of such a wide river would have been a very public matter, and a disguise as pilgrims might not have been enough to allay a worrying curiosity on the part of onlookers. Worrying indeed, for Etheldreda would have remained unaware of Egfrid's surrender to the elements, and always in her mind would have been the possibility of capture.

For this reason Etheldreda's small party, though using the Roman road as a navigational guide, kept a few miles to the west of it, and tracked tortuously from village to village, where the people would accept them as pilgrims – pilgrims who had perhaps lost their way – and extend to them food and shelter. One such village was 'Alftham', now West Halton near Winteringham, just south of the Humber river. It seems that Etheldreda had met, years before on her northern journey, a local chieftain, and her party was able to take refuge in his hall within the folds of the sandy wooded hills. In gratitude, we are told, she built the villagers a church. This may be taken to mean that she marked out a place of worship and promised to finance the church, leaving its construction to take place after she had gone on her way. (One may here conjecture whether the party took with them a small stone tablet, religiously inscribed, and used it as a travelling altar.)

Still unsure of themselves, and perhaps made aware that they could be taken in for questioning by armed men loyal to Egfrid (remembering that Lindsey had been – at least nominally – in his possession until a short time earlier), wearily they carried on towards Lincoln, and thence to the Sleaford district. Now they could breathe more easily as they came to country firmly under the control of the Mercian king, Wulfhere, and perhaps at last they could resume their monastic attire.

Once Etheldreda had become a nun she qualified, in the eyes of the chroniclers, for miraculous happenings. On this journey there were two miracles. The first, south of Coldingham, where the sea was said to have unaccountably raged in a manner sufficient to deter Egfrid and his thanes, has already been described. The second, and best known, is the sprouting of a staff which Etheldreda stuck into the ground preparatory to sleeping. When she awoke next morning the ash wood staff had produced buds, and even new leaves.

It is not too difficult to imagine how this story could have arisen. It is well known that a stick of willow, pressed into the soil, will in fact sprout quite rapidly and in due course grow into a tree. Indeed substantial willow hedges have been established in this way. It is true that Etheldreda's staff was said to have been ash, not willow, but with the passage of time the two could have been confused, either by accident or design. The likelihood is that Etheldreda was using a staff of the ubiquitous willow rather than ash, and later, because ash trees were, and remain, very prevalent along this part of her route, there came the assumption that the tree was in fact an ash. Clearly no stick would sprout overnight, and the likelihood is that that Etheldreda and her companions settled into a small community for three or four weeks, either because the weather was bad or simply to take much needed rest – for after all there was no longer any great urgency surrounding the journey – and the stick was totally forgotten until the time came to return to the spot – probably a cross-roads – and resume the journey.

It may be that the miracle of the budding staff took place at the old horse-trading field by the crossroads of Stow near Threekingham.

Something should be said about the location of the miracle, since there are two candidates. One of these is the village of Stow-in-Lindsey, eight miles northwest of Lincoln; from Stow the great cathedral is easily visible. The alternative is at Threekingham, much further south along the journey, and northeast of Sleaford.

Until recently the northern Stow has been generally regarded as the most likely. Its church, now St Mary's, used to be the church of St Etheldreda's Stow. However Stow – 'place' – is a common name, widely dispersed across some parts of England. This site is about six miles west of Ermine Street, and just off a secondary Roman road to Lincoln. It may be that the party still thought it prudent not to use the main highway, even at a distance of thirty miles from the Humber. Lincoln may well have been their immediate destination; keeping a low profile, they could have found food and shelter within the extensive Roman ruins, now thinly repopulated by Anglo-Saxons. But it is possible, given their continuing suspicions, that they opted to stay clear of the city, riding in only to obtain food supplies.

We now come to the alternative place, again called Stow. In point of fact this Stow is too small to be marked on most maps. It is no more than a crossroads on Ermine Street a few miles south of Sleaford,and certainly on Etheldreda's direct route to the Peterborough area. This would have been a quite feasible stopping point, the more so since a grassy mound at the crossroads was the site of a medieval horse-fair. If this market went back to long before medieval times – as it well may have done – then the fair, itself only yearly, would have given rise to a permanent collection of hutments and stables where travellers would have halted not only to change horses but also to make numerous essential purchases. There would have been hostelries, food stalls, and so on. The crossroads would have been the equivalent of today's motorway service station. It is not stretching the imagination unduly to see Etheldreda and the others staying there – perhaps in an encampment – for several days or even weeks, and perhaps long enough for a staff of willow to burst its buds. So this second alternative, the virtually unnamed Stow near Threekingham in south Lincolnshire, seems to have the edge.

Drawing ever nearer to her home country, and well rested and refreshed, Etheldreda would now have begun to take some pleasure in the journey. She had, for the first time in her life, faced physical danger and come through it, and she would never again be the same person as when she fled in fear from the abbey at Coldingham. There was much she had to do when she reached her island, but for the present she could revel in the spring weather and amble gently but surely towards Ely. (If the story of the budding staff is to be believed we can use the knowledge that the willow is one of the earliest trees to break bud to deduce that the time was late March or early April.)

The continuing road would lead Etheldreda and her friends to the old Roman settlement, now in ruins, at Castor, west of what is now Peterborough but was then the monastery of Medehamstede, founded nearly twenty years earlier by the then king of Mercia, Penda's Christian son Peada. Here it is likely that she would have visited the great abbey and there developed some first thoughts towards the founding of a monastery of her own. That at Medehamstede may have taken many years to build, as it was consecrated by the Archbishop of Canterbury only in 665.

The long journey southward took Etheldreda and her few companions along secret and often perilous ways through woodland and thicket.

From Medehamstede Etheldreda would have passed through a gently rolling countryside heavily wooded with oak trees, and then turned southeast at Godmanchester along the Via Devana. Finally the party would have struck north into light woodland and bushes, with a scatter of small settlements, open glades, and a modicum of tillage on the flat gravels around Willingham. Where this hard land petered out she would have been able to see at long last her own homeland across no more than a mile of misty fenland, lying very wet at the end of winter but still negotiable with the knowledge of Ovin or of a local guide. In short she would have retraced the steps of that distant time when, full of apprehension but buoyed by her great faith, she had left Cratendune for an unknown future in Northumbria.

So at last Etheldreda had returned home to her beloved island in the fens. She was forty three years old, and had spent fourteen years in the distant north. Now there was much to be done, and no one could foresee how little time she would have in which to do it.

14

THE MONASTIC FOUNDATION

From the settlement at Braham could be seen the unpeopled hill more than a mile to the north, a fitting place for Etheldreda to build a great monastery.

One can hardly imagine the ethereal joy Etheldreda would have experienced on seeing again, after fourteen long years, her much-loved island rising out of the reedy pools of the fenland. As she and her companions wound their tortuous way across the mile or so of swampland, seeking out mounds and tufts of spongy grass amid the tangle of thicket and sedge, and finding someone to pole them across the waters sluggishly seeping their way through the midst of the wasteland, her mind would have returned to that day when, with Ovin and her own devoted followers, she embarked on the journey to a strange northern land of moors, stark headlands, and cold, sparkling waters of lake and rill – a far cry from the soft landscapes of her childhood days and her early years as a young woman.

Fittingly, the first place they would have come to once they set foot on firm land was Ovin's own village of Haddenham. Now Etheldreda had just six or seven miles to traverse before reaching what remained of the tiny church she herself had founded within the village of Cratendune, by the bank of the broad winding river which at this spring season of the year would have been in its fullest and most majestic flow.

However wearisome the journey had been, Etheldreda must now have been bursting with an enthusiasm to repair the church, resume her companionship with those who still remained of her original community, and gather others into her haven. But also nagging away at her would have been the fact that she was now a consecrated nun, as were Sewenna and Sewara, with Ovin changed from steward to monk, and that between them they ought to produce something more significant than a simple wood-and-thatch hutment containing an altar. She had dwelt in an abbey at Coldingham and, one may believe, walked and prayed in the great stone-built monastery at Medehamstede. So her ambitions would have been set very high and brought her to meditating in her waking hours, and perhaps even in her dreams, on the possibilities of creating something akin to what she had already seen. And she would never have forgotten the example of her friend and mentor, Abbess Hilda of Whitby, and the lasting successes this great woman had achieved.

Moreover there was the tradition that a royal person would found a monastery as a mark of gratitude to God. King Oswy, for instance, created no fewer than twelve such monasteries – Oswy never did things by halves – after he had defeated Penda in battle. Etheldreda was the daughter of a king, and a princess of the South Girvii. She had survived a dangerous journey and would have yearned to express in tangible form her great thankfulness for divine protection.

All these thoughts must have occupied her mind and time to such an extent that she felt an urgent need to put her ideas into effect. But she had no notion of how to set about it. Neither she nor Ovin knew the first thing about constructing a building of any magnitude, and there was no one on the island whom she could ask. So what was she to do?

The greatest builder of the seventh century was Wilfrid, now at the zenith of his powers as Archbishop of York. He it was who constructed the abbeys at Hexham and Ripon with their remarkable crypts, and it was Wilfrid the restless traveller who moved around unceasingly as he supervised the building of new centres of worship here, there and everywhere, but especially in newly Christian Mercia. Heartily disliked by Egfrid's new wife Eormenburga, Wilfrid had discretion enough to spend most of the time south of the Humber, and he now visited Etheldreda and discussed with her the creation of a new monastery on her island. But there is every reason to believe that the idea of building such a monastery was Etheldreda's alone, and that Wilfrid's role was to provide the moral and technical support she needed to boost her confidence in such an formidable undertaking.

The island of Ely (it has to be remembered that Ely itself did not then exist, except perhaps as a few scattered hutments by the hillside springs) was akin to fenland islets such as Thorney, Crowland and Chatteris in being accessible only with difficulty from the world outside, and therefore through their very remoteness ideal for religious pursuits. This does not mean that monasteries and nunneries did not make visitors welcome – hospitality was indeed a major function and duty – nor that communities would be discouraged from developing around them. The way of life of monks and nuns was based – though perhaps not in formal terms – on the Benedictine way of living, and this included much dealing with lay people. But such isolated settlements would be least subjected to the influences and possible interference of noblemen of the courts, ambitious entrepreneurs, and indeed military adventurers. A remote community would be able to develop in its own way and at its own pace.

The monastery was located a little to the south of the present cathedral, by the springs feeding the small streamlet which trickled down into the fenland pools.

Thus, with her recollections of the Cratendune community to draw on, and with the strong encouragement of her friend and long-time adviser Wilfrid, Etheldreda would have needed little convincing of the suitability of the island for monastic development.

But such a far-reaching project would be enormously expensive, particularly if the abbey were to follow the example of Wilfrid's northern buildings and be made – at least as far as the walls were concerned – of stone. The geology of the island precluded the inclusion of a crypt, and from the point of view of cost it was perhaps just as well that this option was not open to Wilfrid, whose imagination, when allowed to do so, would run riot. There is no true building stone on the island, which consists of clay with here and there a capping of sand. Only in the few places where the sand is cemented by iron can it be used for any kind of building, with the outcome weak and readily weathered. The nearest good building material, a limestone, was in Saxon as well as later times quarried in pits owned by the abbey of Medehamstede, and good relations between monasteries, whether existing or potential, did not extend to financial generosity; any stone would have to be paid for.

In addition to this the heavy stone blocks would have to be moved some forty miles to the island, and the only practicable means was by water. Fortunately the waterway system was extensive enough for this to be done, but the cost of transport would be very considerable and would add substantially to the expense. So Wilfrid may well have expressed doubts about the proposal.

It was therefore a matter of extreme good fortune that it was now Etheldreda's cousin Aldulf who had succeeded her uncle as ruler of East Anglia. Aldulf was about the same age as his cousin, and a convinced Christian. Also East Anglia had now, after the vicissitudes of war and conquest, become rich and prosperous, not only in monetary wealth but in many ideas brought from the mainland of Europe. Wilfrid was always interested in ideas, but at present it was material wealth that occupied his thinking: who could pay for the great abbey he was to build for Etheldreda? We do not know what pressures were brought to bear, but it is a fact that Wilfrid was exceptionally persuasive. Suffice it to say that Aldulf was prepared – indeed anxious – to finance the foundation of what was to be a very substantial monastery.

Everything was now in place – or so it seemed. The brimming river flowed close to the island at one point only, at the settlement of Braham/Cratendune, and this is where the stone could be unloaded from the barges, and the monastery duly constructed there on the site of Etheldreda's church.

This is however where Etheldreda showed what some call determination, and others less charitably call stubbornness. Whatever its true definition, it evidenced her new found confidence. As time went on she became adamant that the abbey should be built, not at Cratendune, but on the near-deserted hill more than a mile to the north, on land now occupied by the southern buildings of Ely's cathedral.

Why did she choose this position? The historians say simply that it was a site 'nearer the river'. But this could not have been so. The course of the river at that time brought it across from the foot of Stuntney hill, a marshy mile from the shore of Eel Island.

The answer must surely be that Etheldreda wanted her abbey to be as near to heaven as possible, however difficult it might be to effect this. The hill at Ely is not the very highest part of the island – that is the ridge where stands Ovin's own village of Haddenham and on which he himself may have built a church on his return – but it is a very prominent feature. Moreover – and here Etheldreda must have conceded that practical considerations could not be entirely ignored – it was not too far from the unloading dock at Braham, and equally not calculated to place too great a burden on all the people who would wish to leave Cratendune and move to the new site.

There are those who consider that Cratendune stood high on the hill to the west of Braham, and we looked earlier at the pros and cons. But one further point may now be made: why would Etheldreda wish to move from one hill to another only triflingly higher, with its crest a half-mile further from a river now lying across treacherous fens? Throughout this story of Etheldreda's life we have been trying to work out a narrative which, on the balance of possibilities thrown up by the evidence, best holds together. If the church of Cratendune was indeed on a hilltop visible for miles around it is more than probable that Wilfrid could have persuaded Etheldreda to build her abbey there.

However if the village of Cratendune was on a mound of land just above the river-bank at Braham, it is easy to see why this would not have suited Etheldreda. It has been said earlier that the Saxons sited their major settlements on a low hill, well drained and not far from a source of good fresh water, with a food supply in the form of fish and water fowl. Etheldreda grew to womanhood in this sort of environment at both Exning and Rendlesham, and Felix's monastery at Soham was similarly placed close to the mere – though it has to be said that the Soham hill is a barely perceptible one. Then as time went on, she lived – however unhappily – at the splendidly sited stronghold at Bamburgh, and thence moved into the cliff top monastery of Coldingham. She would probably have seen and been much impressed by Hilda's great abbey on another cliff at Whitby. The only time she had lived at a really low altitude was when she was at Cratendune, and although she had been perfectly contented there, all these recollections, and especially those of childhood, were bound to have remained with her. So, with this kind of background, and given the other considerations already referred to, it is not surprising that she was becoming restless by the riverside and would have preferred to build her new church on some more elevated land.

On the other hand one has to remember that Etheldreda, despite these desires, was at this time a very worn-out person indeed. She had endured many years of hopeless frustration, followed by a brief interlude at Coldingham which had culminated in the trauma of the escape and the arduous journey southward. Despite all her aspirations, and her experiences of great monasteries elsewhere, her physical and mental – though certainly not her spiritual – exhaustion must have tempted her to accept that the enlargement of the Cratendune church was as much as she could manage, at least for the foreseeable future.

What signalled to Etheldreda that the time had indeed come to erect a hill top monastery? There is a plausible answer to this, but to put it forward we have to revisit the kingdom of Kent, and specifically the Isle of Sheppey, where within the geographical island a marked hill – higher that Ely's own – rises out of the erstwhile marshes.

When Seaxburga's husband died of the plague in 664 their son was too young to assume the reins of kingship, and Seaxburga acted for a time as regent. After a few years the boy became king, and rewarded his mother with a grant of land at Sheppey on which to build an abbey for seventy-seven nuns. Seaxburga now founded this nunnery and became its first abbess. But in 673 – the year Etheldreda returned to Ely – the young king died. Seaxburga, who seems to have been particularly close to her son, must have been heartbroken. Knowing that her devoted younger sister had returned home, would not Seaxburga have made the journey to Ely to see and talk with her after their long separation? And would she not have told about the foundation on the hill at Sheppey, and – as so often in their past – given Etheldreda the impetus, spiced with good practical sense, to put her inspiration into practice?

For the resemblance of the Saxon site at Minster on Sheppey to that at Ely is a remarkable one: both steeply overlooking marshes, both with available drinking water either from wells or springs, both including readily cultivable land. Looking across the marshland towards Minster is very much like looking at Ely's island. Was the Saxon abbey at Minster indeed the model on which Etheldreda's monastery was based, and did the ever-helpful Seaxburga give Etheldreda the final impulse to contact Wilfrid and begin its construction?

We have noted that Wilfrid might have had – at least initially – practical reservations but, with or without his full approval, the monastery came to be built immediately south of the site of the present cathedral.

The building would have taken some years to complete, but could doubtless have functioned as a place of worship long before that. Unlike that at Sheppey, this was a 'double monastery' (the first in the south of England) after the style of Coldingham and Whitby, where nuns – who were the majority – and monks lived separately and came together in music and prayer, while a monk would conduct the services. Such monasteries were invariably headed by an abbess, often of royal blood, and she stamped her own character on the foundation. We are told little about Etheldreda's management of her own monastery, other than that she was an excellent abbess who commanded not only the respect, but also the full affection, of those around her – her nuns and monks certainly, but also the lay people in the village of Ely which soon grew up around the monastery. We do know that a chaplain named Huna came to Ely to organise the sacramental life of the abbey, and that he himself became very devoted to her.

Wilfrid himself seems to have taken a special interest in this foundation. He not only officiated when Etheldreda was made abbess, but managed to obtain for her monastery a number of special privileges, including exemptions from royal jurisdiction. Clearly Wilfrid remained closely attached to Etheldreda right up to her death, but he was fated to be in Rome when she actually died. She had seen her abbey become one of the greatest in England, noted not only for its religious devotions and its chanting, but also for its embroidery and other craft work, and its education of young people. There can be no doubts that Etheldreda's fullest hopes had now been realised, and although she had only seven years as head of her foundation, they must have been years of the truest fulfilment.

We read a little about Etheldreda as Abbess, but nothing that contributes greatly to an understanding of her character. It is said, for example, that she wore not linen, but woollen garments. This may, or it may not, have been unusual in a seventh-century Saxon monastery. It is stated that she had only three hot baths a year – but abstinence from hot baths other than on the most sacred dates was normal monastic procedure in those days.

Etheldreda had, we are told, just one meal a day except on special days or when because of physical weakness she needed more. But many people today maintain themselves on one basic meal. It is also stated that she always remained in prayer after her nuns and monks had retired to bed, but she cannot have gone without sleep indefinitely. What probably happened was that on special occasions, as when someone died, she would maintain an all-night vigil; the chroniclers, suffused with good intentions, would magnify this into something approaching the miraculous.

One may feel no need for stories of this kind, for it must be abundantly clear from everything in Etheldreda's history that she would have carried out her duties with humility and total religious devotion. Her care for her charges is abundantly evident from the grief they showed when she died, and from Seaxburga's subsequent translation of her sister's body from the nuns' graveyard, where Etheldreda had humbly chosen to be buried, into a monastic shrine.

Etheldreda's niece Ermenilda became a novice at Ely when her husband Wulfhere was killed in battle by Egfrid, and she later replaced Seaxburga as abbess of the monastery at Sheppey in Kent. Ultimately she became the third Abbess of Ely, but in the meantime Seaxburga – concerned that she had never been trained as a nun – came to Ely as a novice under Etheldreda. The devotion of Seaxburga to her younger sister has been commented on in the earlier parts of this story, and the fact that it lasted, firm and unbroken, from birth to death is an undying tribute to both sisters. When Etheldreda died Seaxburga succeeded her, and brought the abbey to its fullest glory in the twenty years during which she was its abbess. On Seaxburga's own death in her seventies in 699 Ermenilda returned from Sheppey, and then Ermenilda's daughter, the well known and much celebrated Werburga, followed her mother, so that the first four abbesses formed an unbroken family line.

Once again, and now finally, an episode in this story concludes with a reference to Ovin. Ovin's name, in people's minds, is second only to that of Etheldreda herself. Tonbert, Egfrid, Ebba may not always be household names, but the faithful steward Ovin is universally known as part of her history. What became of Ovin?

Along this ancient way passed generation upon generation, and here Etheldreda must have journeyed many times to meet Ovin, her steward and her great friend.

It is the belief, based on tangible evidence, that Ovin returned – most probably with Etheldreda herself – to the island, and in his own village of Haddenham built, at its highest point, a church. Whether he founded a religious community cannot be known, but if Ovin was solitary by nature his church was possibly no more than a small oratory used for private prayer. But it does seem clear that Ovin was highly regarded locally. He had been the island's steward under its princess, and had gone north with her many years before. Now, old and grizzled, he had returned to his roots. He must have been a much-loved figure within the village, and it is not surprising that when he died, probably round about 675, a tall cross of stone was erected to his memory.

This cross was probably commissioned and paid for by Etheldreda, who caused an inscription in Latin to be cut on the plinth; in translation it reads 'Give, O God, to Ovin, Thy Light and Rest. Amen'. The cross was, it is thought, placed at the site of the first worship, by a small dip along the ridgeway where the land begins to rise up towards the present church.

If so it was indeed well sited, for as the centuries rolled on and the more intrepid travellers crossed the dank fen to enter the island by the fishing hutments of Aldreth, the newcomers would be welcomed at the hostelries of Haddenham village, and amidst the first lowly buildings they would wonder at the great upstanding cross of Ovin. The cross itself has never been recovered, but the base was brought to Ely by the historian James Bentham in the early years of the nineteenth century and placed in the Cathedral, where it still remains, by far the oldest creation of man within the building.

Etheldreda erected an inscribed monumental cross to her old steward Ovin, and placed it by his own chapel in the village of Haddenham.

Ovin's cross on the hillside.

15

THE PASSING OF ETHELDREDA

In the spring of 679 there swept through England a virulent pestilence, one of the many that shortened so many lives through the centuries. Once the attack had invaded a monastic community it would spread like wildfire, and in June Etheldreda herself was struck down. Particularly painful was a swelling below the jaw, and although it was lanced by the physician Kynefrid and appeared for two days to be free of poison, the relief was only temporary, and Etheldreda's condition worsened until she herself knew that death was imminent.

The chroniclers, Bede included, made a great deal of the last days, or hours, of those much respected for their piety, so that they could be seen as an example to others. Abbess Hilda's illness and death are described in detail, and the fact that Etheldreda received the same degree of attention indicates beyond doubt the reverence in which she was held. The unfeigned sorrow at her impending death is further evidence, if such were needed, of the affection she generated among all sections of her community.

The accounts of deathbed scenes are often a mixture of fact and fiction, the latter frequently with mystical overtones. But the account of Etheldreda's final days bears the ring of truth. Having settled the necessary arrangements within the monastery - and it was quite clear that the successor would be her sister Seaxburga - she spoke cheerfully to her weeping companions about her joy at leaving the world of humans, with all its iniquities, and being received into heaven. She even took pleasure in her painful affliction, saying it was the will of God that she be punished for her vanities as a girl, when she delighted in wearing gold and precious stones around her neck. In short she was showing in the presence of death the same characteristics of humility and courage as she had in life, and we can find no difficulty in believing Bede's moving account of her final hours.

Abbess Etheldreda died on the twenty-third of June 679 at the age of forty-nine and was buried, as she wished, in the nuns' graveyard, in a simple coffin of wood.

Etheldreda has been called the most popular of the Saxon saints. One can readily see that her life had a biblical quality about it, which would appeal to great numbers of ordinary people, both in her own time and in succeeding generations. The early dedication of her whole existence to Christ, her first arranged marriage, her retirement from worldly affairs on the death of her husband, her exodus to Northumbria to embark on another marriage, her pleas to be released from court life, her year in the northern monastery, the king's attempt to kidnap her, her dramatic escape, her long and dangerous journey back to her homeland, all these culminating in her final triumph - the narrative alone would fire the imagination of people who could have had no possible conception of what she was like as a person.

All accounts of Etheldreda's life finish in the same way. In 695 Seaxburga, now an old lady, still with a great love in her heart for her younger sister, decreed that Etheldreda's bones be disinterred from the open graveyard and installed in a sanctuary within the monastery so that they could be venerated with proper ceremony. A 'marble' - in fact almost certainly stone - sarcophagus was discovered at Grantchester and floated down-river to Ely. It was recorded that the head-cavity in the stone fitted precisely the contours of Etheldreda'a own head. But most extraordinary of all was the state of her body, which was found to be not only totally uncorrupted, but healed from the poisons which had entered it.

It had been suggested that the body was simply mummified, but this would have presented an unattractive spectacle, impossible to equate with the kind of fresh purity described by Bede. Bede was drawing on material then available to him, including chronicles subsequently lost, but he may also have had a personal testimony from

Wilfrid, who was present at the exhumation. Wilfrid virtually worshipped Etheldreda, in life and death, and one may suggest - albeit somewhat lamely - that he may have simply seen what he wanted to see. Such a story was certainly applied to many sacred people throughout Saxon times; Cuthbert and Withburga are two who come immediately to mind. But it is also said that Etheldreda's left hand - in whatever condition - was rescued from destruction by a devotee when the shrine was desecrated in the reign of Henry the Eighth. The hand was placed in a reliquary, and passed down - indeed by a documented route - through the centuries, so that it is still with us today, desiccated and much darkened with age. The fingers and thumb are curved as if about to pick up something with great delicacy. The most fascinating thing of all is the size of the hand, which is very small, almost childlike.

This last narrative is far from unbelievable. But whatever the truth of these things the story of incorruptibility is one of great beauty, and perhaps a fitting way to bring to a close Etheldreda's quite remarkable, in many ways inspiring, and often very moving story.

Epilogue

It was just a year ago when she died, on a day like this, as the spring turned into summer. Spring can be very cold on this hill with the east winds sweeping across the fens, and summer can be humid and unpleasant with the marsh vapours rising. But now, as I look across the great spaces, I see a placid beauty, and I understand how my sister yearned for this remote island place which she would always call her home.

I was used to the cold winds on my own island at Sheppey, salt-laden and bitterly stinging. I should have told her about the winds of Sheppey, because she always said I was the practical one. Down at Cratendune she was sheltered in the trees. But the Coldingham cliffs must have been bleak and fearsome. I shall never go there, but she told me of her life at the court, and of her agonies of mind, and about those last perilous hours.

Sometimes I wonder whether I did the right thing in arguing that she should go to Northumbria. Everything has come right in the end, but should she have been asked to endure as she did? She clung to that great faith of hers through everything. How she managed to journey home through the bleak moors and the thorn thickets and the dark and fearsome forests I, the practical one, shall never fully understand.

She was the dreaming one, the romantic. She liked to wander alone along the stream, and yet she loved the company of others. Even I could not always understand the thoughts going though my young sister's mind. She turned many things over in those thoughts of hers. She needed to talk about them to someone, and it was usually me. But

I never influenced her as Hilda did. Hilda's visit changed her life for ever.

There was this desire to find the truth of things, to be brought to decisions. And once the important ones had been made I have never seen anyone so single-minded. She had, underneath everything, a will of steel.

I was the practical one, getting married, having children, governing a kingdom. She told me she could never have ruled anybody, even her tiny island. But in six years she built a monastery and governed it wisely and well.

She changed much over the last years. The serene, so positive middle-aged abbess would scarcely have been recognised by the young woman.

I remember her great appeal in those early days. She was trim and small boned, and very neat in her ways. And she seemed unsure of herself, always seeking help and advice. So we all wanted to protect her.

All her life through she inspired loyalty, not just as a princess but because of her great openness and honesty. She was a very emotional person. She wore her heart on her sleeve, and people knew this and were drawn to her because of it.

Of course she herself was utterly loyal, to father and to his kingdom. She put loyalty before everything but her own dedication and faith. So she came over to this island. I know she found real happiness here. Perhaps she should have stayed at Cratendune that first time. But then there would have been no monastery, and she would never have been really fulfilled.

I think she was destined to go through all this pain to show how faith can bring patience and great courage, and lead to that final serenity. And now I have to keep alive all her ideals. She always said I would live to be a hundred. I have kept the strength I was born with, and perhaps this preserved me from the plague that carried her away.

She wanted to be buried in the nuns' graveyard and this is where she has been laid. I see the greensward lying below. But she should be somewhere where people can come to her and pray, somewhere where she is free from the bitter winds of winter and the fen vapours of summer. One day, many years ahead, I will see that this comes to pass.

Dusk is falling upon the land. A small bird has flown in one window and straight out of another. I cannot say what it was. She knew all the birds, every one of them. There was a story about a bird flying into a room and returning to the darkness. For an instant we see it in life, but of the before and after we know nothing. Etheldreda often told that story. Now at last she knows where the bird has gone. But I think she already knew.

The darkness has come, and I must go to pray. Shall I carry a taper? I think not, for there is no need. The abiding light of my sister's presence is with me and will guide me through the night, and it will stay with me all the days of my life.

THE PEOPLE IN THE STORY

Aldulf – Etheldreda's first cousin. King of East Anglia who succeeded Ethelwald.

Alfrid – Oswy's eldest son. Northumbria's sub-king at York.

Anna – King of East Anglia and father of Etheldreda.

Cuthbert – Prior of Lindisfarne.

Eanfleda – Wife of Oswy.

Ebba – Sister of Oswy, and Abbess of Coldingham.

Egfrid – Son of Oswy. Prince, later King, of Northumbria and Etheldreda's second husband.

Egric – Anna's elder brother and Sigbert's cousin. Became King of East Anglia on Sigbert's abdication.

Eormenburga – Egfrid's mistress, and later his wife.

Eorpwald – Redwald's son and successor.

Erconbert – Husband of Seaxburga. King of Kent.

Ermenilda – Daughter of Seaxburga. Wulfhere's wife, and Queen of Mercia. Third Abbess of Ely.

Ethelburga – Daughter of Anna.

Etheldreda – Princess of East Anglia and the island of Ely, Queen of Northumbria, first Abbess of Ely.

Ethelhere – Anna's brother and successor.

Ethelwald – Etheldreda's uncle, who succeeded Ethelhere.

Felix – First Bishop of East Anglia.

Fursey – Irish monk and mystic, who came to East Anglia in the reign of Sigbert.

Hereswith – Widow of Egric, retired to French monastery.

Hilda – Abbess of Whitby.

Huna – Etheldreda's chaplain at Ely.

Iurminus – Anna's son.

Kynefrid – Etheldreda's physician.

Oswy – King of Northumbria, Overlord of the English Kingdoms.

Ovin – Etheldreda's steward and governor of the island of Ely.

Peada – Son of Penda, who married one of Oswy's daughters and converted to Christianity. Succeeded Penda as King of Mercia.

Penda – Chieftain and later King of Mercia.

Redwald – King of East Anglia at Rendlesham.

Seaxburga – Anna's daughter (Etheldreda's older sister). Second Abbess of Ely.

Sethryd – Anna's step-daughter.

Sewara and Sewenna – Etheldreda's companions when she left Northumbria.

Sigbert – Son of Redwald, exiled to France. Later King of East Anglia.Abdicated to become a monk.

Tonbert – Alderman or Prince, of the island of Ely, and first husband of Etheldreda.

Werburga – Daughter of Ermenilda. Fourth Abbess of Ely.

Wilfrid – Bishop of York.

Withburga – Anna's youngest daughter.

Wulfhere – King of Mercia after Penda and Peada. Ermenilda's husband.

CHRONOLOGY

Some dates are definite; others are deduced from the available evidence

597	Augustine lands at Thanet in Kent and converts King Ethelbert.
605	Death of Augustine.
616	Ethelbert of Kent dies, and is succeeded as Overlord of the English Kingdoms (Bretwalda) by Redwald of East Anglia.
624	Death of Redwald; he is succeeded by the pagan Eorpwald.
626	Penda becomes King of Mercia.
627	Eorpwald converted to Christianity.
628	On Eorpwald's death, East Anglia reverts to paganism.
630	Sigbert, a Christian, secures the kingship of East Anglia. Etheldreda born at Exning.
634	Wilfrid and Cuthbert born.
635	Foundation of monastery at Lindisfarne.
636	Bishop Felix arrives at Felixstowe and establishes a monastery and school at Dunwich. Fursey in East Anglia at Burgh Castle.
639	Sigbert abdicates to become a monk; succeeded by Egric.
640	Erconbert becomes King of Kent. Penda invades East Anglia, and kills Sigbert and Egric. Anna becomes King of East Anglia.
641/2	Erconbert marries Princess Seaxburga.

647   Hilda of Northumbria stays at Anna's court, and then returns to Northumbria.
Death of Bishop Felix.

652   Etheldreda marries Tonbert of the island of Ely.

654   Penda's second invasion of East Anglia. Anna and his son killed at Bulcamp. Ethelhere becomes King.

655   Penda and Ethelhere killed by Oswy at battle of Winwaed.
Ethelwald now King of East Anglia.
Tonbert dies.
Etheldreda appoints Ovin as governor of the island of Ely, and establishes a religious community at Cratendune.
Peada, son of Penda, now King of Mercia.

656   Peada baptised. Murdered the same year.

658   Wulfhere secures Kingdom of Mercia.

659   Seaxburga's daughter Ermenilda marries Wulfhere.
Etheldreda goes to Northumbria and marries Egfrid.

664   Erconbert of Kent dies in plague.
Egfrid becomes sub-king of Deira at York.

665   Cuthbert becomes Prior of Lindisfarne.

669   Wilfrid Bishop of York.
Monastery of Medehamstede (Peterborough) consecrated.
Somewhere about this time Seaxburga founded her abbey at Minster on the Isle of Sheppey.

670   Death of Oswy. Egfrid King of Northumbria.

672   Etheldreda retires to Coldingham monastery.

673   Etheldreda flees Coldingham and returns to Cratendune.
Monastery at Ely commenced.

674   Wulfhere killed in a battle with Egfrid. Ermenilda becomes a nun at Ely.

675   Ovin dies.

679   Etheldreda dies at Ely on 23 June. Succeeded as Abbess by Seaxburga.

680   Death of Hilda.

685   Egfrid killed in ambush by Picts.

695   Translation of Etheldreda's body into the monastery at Ely on 17 October.

699   Death of Seaxburga. Succeeded by her daughter Ermenilda, widow of Wulfhere. (Ermenilda was succeeded, at a date unknown, by her daughter Werburga.)

870   Monastic buildings destroyed by Danes, but ruins continue to be used for Christian worship.

970   Monastery restored by Dunstan; remains until dismantled by King William in 1083.

1083   Norman monastery commenced.

1109   Abbey Church becomes Cathedral of new Diocese of Ely. Abbot becomes first Bishop.

Bamburgh	seat of the Northumbrian kings
Blythburgh	site of King Anna's church by Suffolk coast
Bulcamp	a hill near Blythburgh, on which Anna was killed
Braham	likely site of Cratendune on Ely's island
Burgh Castle	Roman fort by River Yare, occupied by Fursey
Bury St Edmunds	monastic site with shrine of Iurminus
Coldingham	Northumbrian abbey, Etheldreda's destination
Canterbury	seat of kings of Kent
Cratendune	Saxon name of Etheldreda's place of seclusion
Dunwich	Suffolk monastery and school of Bishop Felix
East Dereham	mid-Norfolk site of Withburga's convent
Ely	site of Etheldreda's monastery
Exning	Etheldreda's birthplace in west Suffolk
Faremoutiers	in Brie in France, where Sethryd and Ethelburga became abbesses
Felixstowe	Bishop Felix's landing-place, Suffolk coast
Haddenham	Ovin's village on the island of Ely
Hexham	monastery of Wilfrid
Holkham	Withburga's childhood home on Norfolk coast
Lastingham	site of monastery in Yorkshire, entered by Ovin
Lichfield	Mercian Christian centre
Lincoln	Roman city re-peopled by Anglo-Saxons
Lindisfarne	monastery of Northumbrian bishops

London	trading centre in kingdom of Essex
Medehamstede	site of monastery later called Peterborough
Minster	Seaxburga's abbey on isle of Sheppey
Rendlesham	seat of East Anglian kings near Woodbridge
Ripon	monastery of Wilfrid
Soham	Saxon monastery in Cambridgeshire destroyed by Danes
Stow	village near Lincoln, possible site of miracle of Etheldreda's staff
Tamworth	seat of Mercian kings
Threekingham	near Sleaford, alternative site of Etheldreda's miracle
West Halton	by the Humber, Etheldreda's place of sanctuary on the journey south
Whitby	'double monastery' of Hilda
York	seat of king of Deira (sub-king of Northumbria)

PRINCIPAL SOURCES OF WRITTEN INFORMATION

Attwater D   *A Dictionary of Saints* (1938)

Bailey R N   *Saint Wilfrid's Crypts at Ripon and Hexham* (1993)

Bede   *The Ecclesiastical History of the English People*;
                    Trans Thomas Stapleton. Ed P Hereford
                    (Oxford 1935)

Bede   *The Ecclesiastical History of the English People.*
                    Trans B Colgrave. Colgrave and Mynors
                    (Oxford 1969)

Bede   *The Ecclesiastical History of the English People*
                    Ed with an introduction by J McClure and
                    R Collins (Oxford 1994)

                    The Anglo-Saxon Chronicle, Trans
                    G Garmonsway (1953)

Bentham J   *The History and Antiquities of the Conventual and
                    Cathedral Church of Ely* (Cambridge 1771)

Stephenson W   Supplement to the above (Norwich 1812)

Blair P H   *Anglo-Saxon England* (1956)

Blair P H   *Roman Britain and Early England* (1963)

Bruce-Mitford R   *Aspects of Anglo-Saxon Archaeology* (1974)

Bruce-Mitford R L S *Saxon Rendlesham. Proceedings of the
                    Suffolk Institute of Archaeology* (1981)

Butler A   *Butler's Lives of the Fathers, Martyrs and
                    Other Principal Saints* (1756)

Butler A   *Lives of the Saints*: revised, edited and
                    supplemented by H Thurston and D Attwater Vol 2
                    (1956)

Campbell J (Ed)   *The Anglo-Saxons* (1982)

Chant K — *The History of Dunwich* (first published by K Davidson 1974)

Clements J H — A *Brief History of Ely and Neighbouring Villages in the Isle* (Ely 1868)

Conybeare E — *History of Cambridgeshire* (1897)

Darby F M — *Medieval Fenland* (Cambridge 1940)

Delaney J J — *Dictionary of Saints* (1982)

Dorman B E — *The Story of Ely and its Cathedral* (1986)

Dowdy M — *The Monastic Setting of Ely* (Ely 1974)

Farmer D H — *The Oxford Book of Saints* (Oxford 1987)

Finberg H P R — *The Formation of England* (1976)

Fisher D J V — *The Anglo-Saxon Age* (1973)

Fowler G — *Cratendune: A Problem of the Dark Ages* Cambridge Arch Soc Vol 41 (1947)

Godfrey C J — *The Church in Anglo-Saxon England* (Cambridge 1962)

Hall D A — *Fenland Project No 10: Cambridgeshire, Isle of Ely and Wisbech, East Anglia Archaeology* (1996)

Hodge C A H & Seale R — *Soils of the District Around Cambridge* (Harpenden 1966)

Hodgkin R H — *A History of the Anglo-Saxons* (Oxford 1952)

Lester G A — *The Anglo-Saxons: How They Lived and Worked* (1976)

Loyn H R — *Anglo-Saxon England and the Norman Conquest* (1962)

Mee A — *Cambridgeshire* (Hodder and Stoughton 1939)

Mee A — *Suffolk* (Hodder and Stoughton 1941)

Miller E — *The Abbey and Bishopric of Ely* (Cambridge 1951)

Miller & Skertchley — *Fenland, Past and Present* (1878)

Quennell M & C — *Everyday Life in Roman and Anglo-Saxon Times* (1959)

Reaney R H — *The Place-Names of Cambridgeshire and the Isle of Ely* (Cambridge 1943)

Ridyard S J — *The Royal Saints of Anglo-Saxon England* (Cambridge 1988)

Rowland T H — *Anglo-Saxon Northumbria* (1973)

Salway P & Blair J — *The Oxford History of Britain: Roman and Anglo-Saxon Britain* (Oxford 1984)

Seale R S — *Soils of the Ely District* (Harpenden 1975)

Skertchley S B J — *The Geology of Fenland* (1877)

Stenton F M — *Anglo-Saxon England* (Oxford 1943)

Stranks C J — *St Etheldreda, Queen and Abbess* (Ely Cathedral Monograph 1975)

Tierney M A — *Dodd's Church History of England Vol 1* (1839)

Liber Eliensis, by Thomas, a 12th century Monk of Ely

Thomson T D — *Coldingham Priory (1972)*

Whitelock D — *The Beginnings of English History* (1952)

The Victoria County History of Cambridgeshire and the Isle of Ely (Oxford 1938)

Smaller works

Cook M   *The Story of Saint Withburga*
(Dereham Antiquarian Society)

Mundahl-Harris S   *St Hilda and her Times* (Caedmon of Whitby 1997)

Thomson T D   *Coldingham Priory (1972)*

Church of St Etheldreda, West Halton
(extract from the *Hull Times* 1913)

The Royal Ancient and Monastic Parish Church
of St Paul, Jarrow (Visitors' Guide)

*A Brief Guide to the Medieval Chapel of St
Etheldreda*, Ely Place, London (Visitors' Guide)

Exning St Martin (Visitors' Guide)

Holy Trinity, Blythburgh (Visitors' Guide)

Peterborough Cathedral (Pitkin Guide 1990)

Dissolution of the Monasteries (Pitkin Guide 1993)

Minster Abbey, Isle of Sheppey (Visitors' Guide)

St Etheldreda, Queen and Abbess
(Hexham Abbey Visitors' Guide)

Saint Mary's, Stow-in-Lindsey (Visitors' Guide)

Sutton Hoo (Visitors' Guide)

English Historical Review: *King Ethelhere and the
Battle of Winwaed* (1968)

INDEX

In this index E = Etheldreda